Qur'anic Wonders

An explanation of priceless moral reflections from selected verses of the Holy Qur'ān

By
Shaykh Mufti Saiful Islām

JKN Publications

© Copyright by JKN Publications

First Published in January 2020
ISBN 978-1-909114-42-5

British Library Cataloguing in Publication Data. A catalogue record for this book is available from the British Library.

All Rights Reserved. No part of this book may be reproduced, stored in a retrieval system or transmitted in any form or by any means, electronic, mechanical, photocopying, recording or otherwise without the prior permission of the copyright owner.

Publisher's Note:
Every care and attention has been put into the production of this book. If however, you find any errors they are our own, for which we seek Allāh's ﷻ forgiveness and the reader's pardon.

Published by:

JKN Publications
118 Manningham Lane
Bradford
West Yorkshire
BD8 7JF
United Kingdom

t: +44 (0) 1274 308 456 | w: www.jkn.org.uk | e: info@jkn.org.uk

Book Title: Qur'anic Wonders

Author: Shaykh Mufti Saiful Islām

"In the Name of Allāh ﷻ, the Most Beneficent, the Most Merciful"

Contents

Introduction ……………………………………………	6
Calling Unto Allāh ﷻ …………………………………	9
Uniqueness of the Arabic Language …………………	12
Immediate Recognition ………………………………	15
Safety from Seduction …………………………………	16
Regret on Judgement Day ……………………………	22
Enjoining Good & Forbidding Evil …………………	25
Upholding Promises …………………………………	28
Kind Treatment to Parents ……………………………	30
How Many Youngsters? ………………………………	34
Etiquettes of Supplication ……………………………	38
Absence of Tears ………………………………………	40
Different Levels of Salāh ……………………………	42
The Successful Believers ……………………………	45
How Long Did We Live For? …………………………	58
Modesty …………………………………………………	61
The Blame Game ………………………………………	68
The Worldly Life ………………………………………	69
Conviction Upon a Verse ……………………………	71
Sad State of Affairs ……………………………………	74
Signs of Allāh ﷻ ………………………………………	75
Wisdom of Luqmān ……………………………………	81
Knowledge of the Unseen ……………………………	84

The Seal of All Prophets	**89**
Manners ... ... …..	**91**
Status of the Holy Prophet ﷺ	**93**
Nikāh and Taqwa	**99**
Trust Assigned to Humans	**101**

Introduction

All praises are due to Allāh ﷻ Who has bestowed the blessed knowledge of His Exalted Book upon the hearts of His pious servants and Who has made the Holy Qur'ān a source of enlightenment and mercy for the believers. May peace and salutations be upon the last of the Messengers and Prophets - our beloved Prophet Muhammad ﷺ, upon his noble Companions ؓ and upon those who follow their noble lifestyle.

Imām Ghazāli ؒ states that the Holy Qur'ān is a love letter from the Creator to the creation. If one truly loves their beloved, they will make immense effort in trying to understand every word their beloved will utter. In a similar manner, the Holy Qur'ān is the speech of our beloved Lord, thus we should make earnest effort to apprehend its elegance and eloquence. Allāh ﷻ says in the Holy Qu'rān,

كِتَٰبٌ أَنزَلْنَٰهُ إِلَيْكَ مُبَٰرَكٌ لِّيَدَّبَّرُوٓا۟ ءَايَٰتِهِۦ وَلِيَتَذَكَّرَ أُو۟لُوا۟ ٱلْأَلْبَٰبِ

"This is a blessed Book which We have revealed to you (O Muhammad) so that the people may reflect upon its verses and so that the men of understanding i.e. the knowledgeable, take heed." (38:29)

Once we are able to understand the mighty speech of our beloved Lord, only then will we be able to ponder over its meaning and take heed from what has been mentioned. In addition, if we are able to comprehend the speech of Allāh ﷻ, it will allow us to enjoy reading the Holy Qur'ān.

One must make every effort to act upon and instil the teachings of the Holy Qur'ān. This will only be attained once we familiarise ourselves with the Holy Qur'ān, as we will come to learn the laws of our Sharī'ah (Islamic Law) and how to implement this in our lives.

It is very unfortunate that we have become completely neglectful in regularly reciting the Holy Qur'ān when there are so many rewards we could potentially gain. Sayyidunā Abū Umāmah ؓ narrates that he once heard the Messenger of Allāh ﷺ say,

اِقْرَءُوا الْقُرْآنَ فَإِنَّهُ يَأْتِيْ يَوْمَ الْقِيَامَةِ شَفِيْعًا لِأَصْحَابِهٖ

"Recite the Qur'ān, as on the Day of Judgement it will become the means of intercession for its companion." (Muslim)

The science of Tafsīr within itself is very vast, hence the compilation of these specific verses provides the reader with a simple and brief commentary. It is aimed to equip the reader with a small glimpse of the profound beauty of the Holy Qur'ān so that they can gain the passion to study further in depth. It is hoped that this will become a means of encouragement to increase the zeal and enthusiasm to recite and inculcate the teachings of the Holy Qur'ān into our daily lives.

May Allāh ﷻ accept this work, instil the true love of the Holy Qur'ān within our hearts and make this book a means of guidance for the scholars and masses of this Ummah. Āmīn!

(Shaykh Mufti) Saiful Islām
Principal of Jāmiah Khātamun Nabiyeen, Bradford, UK
August 2019/Dhul Qa'dah 1440

Calling Unto Allāh ﷻ

وَإِذَا سَأَلَكَ عِبَادِيْ عَنِّيْ فَإِنِّيْ قَرِيْبٌ أُجِيْبُ دَعْوَةَ الدَّاعِ إِذَا دَعَانِ فَلْيَسْتَجِيْبُوْا لِيْ وَلْيُؤْمِنُوْا بِيْ لَعَلَّهُمْ يَرْشُدُوْنَ

"And when My servants ask you (O Muhammad) about Me, then (tell them that) I am indeed near. I respond to the call of the one when he calls upon Me. So let them respond to Me and believe in Me so that they may be (rightly) guided." (2:186)

According to the sequence of the verse, it should be, وَإِذَا سَأَلَكَ عِبَادِيْ فَقُلْ لَهُمْ إِنِّيْ قَرِيْبٌ "When My servants ask you (O Muhammad) about Me, then tell them that I am indeed near." Allāh ﷻ has taken the Holy Prophet ﷺ out of the equation and stated that now there is direct contact between Him and His servants. Allāh ﷻ says that if His servant asks about Him, He is there; they do not need to go and ask the Holy Prophet ﷺ. They can directly talk to Him whenever they wish.

Allāh ﷻ uses the term إِذَا (when) and not إِنْ (if). The reason is because Allāh ﷻ is optimistic regarding His servants - My servant will supplicate to Me. An example of this is of a mother when sending her son into the military/battlefield. She will not say, "If my son comes back" instead she will say, "When my son comes back" as she has a positive approach i.e. that her son will return home safely.

A question could be posed that as Allāh ﷻ is of a very high status, how can we call unto Him? The answer can be easily understood through an example.

For instance, if there is a Prime Minister or a President present, ordinary citizens will not be able to talk or engage with the Prime Minister or President as they will not have the time to speak to each and every individual. Allāh ﷻ mentions the word عِبَادِيْ (slave) which is of the lowest category. Allāh ﷻ is therefore informing us that even if any one of us are from amongst the lowest category, we still have a direct connection with Allāh ﷻ to implore Him.

The word مُؤْمِنُوْنَ (believers) or اَصْحَابُ (companions) was not mentioned. Allāh ﷻ instead mentions that any person from the slaves who calls upon Him has a direct connection with Him.

Grammatically, the word أُجِيْبُ is on the scale of اِفْعَالُ thus giving the meaning of a prompt reply. Allāh ﷻ is referring to the fact that He instantly replies. When 'My' servant does ask about 'Me', I am always ready for him. Allāh ﷻ did not use the words دُعَا الدَّاعِ but instead used دَعْوَةَ الدَّاعِ. This displays that even if a servant, once in his lifetime calls upon Allāh ﷻ, He will answer. The word دَعْوَةً is the root word (مَصْدَرْ) i.e. the caller's call (even once) when he calls 'Me'. This signifies that every person in the eyes of Allāh ﷻ is Ma'rifah (definite), not Nakirah (indefinite).

If someone has a thousand workers working under his authority and it is said, "The caller called me" (as a proper noun), this is completely different than saying, "A caller called me" (a common noun). In other words, Allāh ﷻ is waiting for everyone who is by definition 'the special one,' to call upon Him so that He may reply immediately.

Aaccording to the grammatical rule, the شَرْط (condition) should be present first and then the جَزَا (outcome) i.e. إِذَا دَعَانِ then أُجِيبُ دَعْوَةَ الدَّاعِ. In this verse, Allāh ﷻ says, "I respond when the caller calls Me" - the جَزَا (outcome) has preceded the شَرْط (condition). This is to demonstrate that Allāh ﷻ is ever-ready to reply, He is ready before we even ask. So, he is saying, "O servant! When are you going to be ready to ask from 'Me'?"

The word اِسْتَجَابَ (Upon the pattern of اِسْتِفْعَالٌ) means that whenever we get the opportunity to call Him, He is ever-ready to answer us—call 'Me' at your own pace and time. When one has made Du'ā and called upon Allāh ﷻ, one may feel that the Du'ā is not being answered. Allāh ﷻ says: I will accept the Du'ā according to My schedule and according to My vast knowledge. Allāh ﷻ knows what is beneficial and harmful for us. For example, if a small child asks the father, "Can I have this knife?" The father will immediately say, 'No' as he knows it can potentially harm the small child. The child may cry and wail for the knife, however, the father knows this is dangerous. In the same way, if the Du'ā isn't accepted, Allāh ﷻ says, وَلْيُؤْمِنُوا بِي ensure that your belief in Allāh ﷻ does not change.

لَعَلَّهُمْ يَرْشُدُونَ - The outcome of doing Duʿā is gaining guidance from Allāh ﷻ.

Lesson: Allāh ﷻ wants us to always make Duʿā to Him and always call unto Him for all our needs. By asking, we will humble ourselves in front of our Lord and become closer to Him. This verse demonstrates that Allāh ﷻ is always ready to answer us no matter what situation we may find ourselves in. We should take this amazing opportunity and regularly make Duʿā for ourselves and others.

Uniqueness of the Arabic Language

الٓرٰ تِلْكَ اٰیٰتُ الْکِتٰبِ الْمُبِیْنِ اِنَّاۤ اَنْزَلْنٰهُ قُرْءٰنًا عَرَبِیًّا لَّعَلَّكُمْ تَعْقِلُوْنَ نَحْنُ نَقُصُّ عَلَیْكَ اَحْسَنَ الْقَصَصِ بِمَاۤ اَوْحَیْنَاۤ اِلَیْكَ هٰذَا الْقُرْاٰنَ وَاِنْ كُنْتَ مِنْ قَبْلِهٖ لَمِنَ الْغٰفِلِیْنَ

"Alif Lām Rā. These are verses of the clear/enlightening book. Indeed, We have sent it down as an Arabic Qurʾān so that you may understand. We narrate to you (O Muhammad) the best of narratives, in what We have revealed to you of this Qurʾān, while before this you were among the unaware." (12:1-3)

This Sūrah was revealed to the Holy Prophet ﷺ during عَامُ الْحُزْن (The year of grief/sorrow). عَامُ الْحُزْن refers to the particular year in which the Holy Prophet's ﷺ beloved wife, Sayyidah Khadījah ؑ and the Holy Prophet's ﷺ beloved uncle, Abū Tālib passed away.

The Arabic language is the most eloquent and articulate language, accomplished in every aspect. Allāmah Imādud-Dīn ﷺ, in his famous work, Tafsīr Ibn Kathīr, mentions under the commentary of this verse,

$$\text{اِنَّا اَنْزَلْنٰهُ قُرْءٰنًا عَرَبِيًّا}$$

"Indeed, We have sent it down as an Arabic Qur'ān so that you may understand." (12:2)

$$\text{اُنْزِلَ أَشْرَفُ الْكُتُبِ بِأَشْرَفِ اللُّغَاتِ عَلٰى أَشْرَفِ الرُّسُلِ بِسِفَارَةِ أَشْرَفِ الْمَلَائِكَةِ وَكَانَ ذٰلِكَ فِيْ أَشْرَفِ بِقَاعِ الْأَرْضِ وَ هُوَ مَكَّةَ وَ اِبْتِدَاءُ اِنْزَالِهٖ فِيْ أَشْرَفِ شُهُوْرِ السَّنَةِ وَهُوَ رَمَضَانُ فَكَمُلَ مِنْ كُلِّ الْوُجُوْهِ}$$

"The most honourable Book was revealed in the most honourable language, to the most honourable Messenger, delivered by the most honourable Angel, in the most honourable land on earth i.e. Makkah and its revelation started during the most honourable month of the year; Ramadhān. Therefore, the Qur'ān is perfect in every angle.

The question could arise as to why the story of Sayyidunā Yūsuf ﷺ is known as أَحْسَنُ الْقَصَصِ (The best of narratives).

The reason is because within the story of Sayyidunā Yūsuf ﷺ, the end result of all the characters e.g. the brothers, father, minister, king etc. are all admirable; the story has a good ending.

The story of Sayyidunā Yūsuf ﷷ and all the other Prophetic stories are mentioned within the previous Holy Books e.g. Tawrāh and Injīl. However, this particular story of Sayyidunā Yūsuf ﷷ has been distorted and understood to the extent of almost as a fairytale and as a love story. Therefore, in the Qur'ān, Allāh ﷻ mentions the true story of Sayyidunā Yūsuf ﷷ clearly and in detail to eradicate all the false notions that were present before. Also, just as the Jews, Polytheists and Christians etc. were all unaware of the true story, Allāh ﷻ says that O Prophet ﷺ, you were also unaware.

<u>Lesson:</u> We should all aspire to learn the Arabic language for three reasons. Firstly, the Holy Qur'ān was revealed in Arabic. Secondly, our beloved Prophet ﷺ was an Arab and spoke Arabic. Thirdly, Arabic will be the language of the people of Jannah (Paradise). If we do not learn Arabic correctly in this world, we will find it difficult to speak with the Hūr of Jannah (Paradise)!

Immediate Recognition

وَقَالَ الَّذِي اشْتَرَاهُ مِنْ مِصْرَ لِامْرَأَتِهِ أَكْرِمِي مَثْوَاهُ عَسَىٰ أَنْ يَنْفَعَنَا أَوْ نَتَّخِذَهُ وَلَدًا

"And the one who bought him from Egypt said to his wife, make his residence comfortable. Perhaps he will benefit us, or, we may adopt him as a son." (12:21)

Historians mention that there are three individuals who were recognised very quickly and became the best physiognomists of the world:

1. The Minister of Egypt recognised the value and excellence of Sayyidunā Yūsuf ﷺ and knew he had exceptional distinct qualities.

2. Sayyidunā Shuaib's ﷺ daughter recognised the value and excellence of Sayyidunā Mūsā ﷺ. She instantly knew he would become a great employee for her father as he possessed the qualities of strength and trustworthiness.

3. Sayyidunā Abū Bakr ﷺ recognised the value and excellence of Sayyidunā Umar ﷺ. During the last moments of Sayyidunā Abū Bakr's ﷺ life, people did not want Sayyidunā Umar ﷺ to become the Caliph as he was very strict. However, Sayyidunā Abū Bakr ﷺ told the Sahābah ﷺ that he is the best person on the earth to fulfill this task after him. He may be stern now but when he receives the burden of Caliphate, he will become of a more gentle nature.

Safety from Seduction

وَرَاوَدَتْهُ الَّتِي هُوَ فِي بَيْتِهَا عَنْ نَفْسِهِ وَغَلَّقَتِ الْأَبْوَابَ وَقَالَتْ هَيْتَ لَكَ قَالَ مَعَاذَ اللهِ إِنَّهُ رَبِّي أَحْسَنَ مَثْوَايَ إِنَّهُ لَا يُفْلِحُ الظَّالِمُونَ

"And she, in whose house he was, sought to seduce him towards herself and bolted/closed the doors and said, "Come towards me." He said (I seek) the refuge of Allāh. Indeed, he (your husband) is my master who has made good my residence. Indeed, the wrongdoers will not succeed." (12:23)

Sayyidunā Yūsuf ﷺ was young and handsome during this stage of his life. It is mentioned within the Aḥādīth of the Holy Prophet ﷺ that Sayyidunā Yūsuf ﷺ was given half of the beauty of this world.

There are two types of beauty:

1. صَبَاحَتْ - A person is immediately dazzled/mesmerised when one lays their eyes upon this certain person/object. This certain type of beauty was possessed by Sayyidunā Yūsuf ﷺ.
2. مَلَاحَتْ - When a person casts their eyes upon this certain person/object, they are captivated and the more they glance, the more they want to continue gazing due to the beauty increasing. This type of beauty was possessed by our beloved Prophet ﷺ.

The word رَبِّيْ could have two possible meanings according to the Scholars of Tafsīr:

1. It could refer to Allāh ﷻ.
2. It could refer to the Minister of Egypt. In Egypt, it was the norm that people would call their master, Rabb (رَبْ).

There were many opportunities present which could have inclined Sayyidunā Yūsuf ﷺ towards seduction e.g. the doors (some Scholars mention there were seven doors in total) were closed and as Sayyidunā Yūsuf ﷺ was her servant, he would reside close to her. Also, being inside a palace would have made it easy to stay together in seclusion. He was also very young at this time, hence it was challenging for Sayyidunā Yūsuf ﷺ to reject. All these avenues could have inclined Sayyidunā Yūsuf ﷺ towards sin. However, he immediately sought refuge in Allāh ﷻ, thus Allāh ﷻ immediately saved him.

وَلَقَدْ هَمَّتْ بِهٖ وَهَمَّ بِهَا لَوْلَا أَنْ رَّاٰ بُرْهَانَ رَبِّهٖ كَذٰلِكَ لِنَصْرِفَ عَنْهُ السُّوْءَ وَالْفَحْشَاءَ إِنَّهٗ مِنْ عِبَادِنَا الْمُخْلَصِيْنَ

"And she certainly determined (to seduce) him and he would have been inclined to her, had he not seen the proof of his Lord. And thus (it was) that We avert from him evil and immorality. Indeed he was one of Our chosen servants." (12:24)

There are five types of thoughts:

1. The thoughts that are present in the mind ceaselessly. This is known as هَاجِسٌ.
2. The thought or thoughts that come into the mind and registers. This is known as خَاطِرٌ.
3. The thought or thoughts that come, registers and speaks with the soul. This is known a حَدِيْثُ النَّفْسِ.
4. The thought or thoughts that come, registers and speaks with the soul and the inclination towards doing the act is present; this can be with regards to righteous or evil actions. If one intends to carry out a good action they will be rewarded. Also, if

a person intends to carry out a sin but refrains, they will also be rewarded with one good deed. This is known as هَمّ.

5. The inclination towards doing the act is present together with the firm intention of carrying out the act. This is known as عَزْمٌ.

The word هَمَّتْ is referring to Zulaikha as there is the female pronoun present here. Also, from the above, we come to notice that Zulaikha had the fourth type of thought (هَمّ). The inclination was present within her to seduce Sayyidunā Yūsuf عليه السلام.

Regarding the phrase وَهَمَّ بِهَا, the Scholars of Tafsīr mention different opinions here:

- Some Scholars are of the opinion that Sayyidunā Yūsuf عليه السلام was not inclined towards Zulaikha at all due to seeing the signs from Allāh جل جلاله.

- Some Scholars opine that Sayyidunā Yūsuf عليه السلام had the intention of committing the sin, but did not perpetrate the act; this resulted in Sayyidunā Yūsuf عليه السلام gaining reward. This can be understood through an example. One may be observing a long fast during the summer season, hence may be inclined towards drinking water. The individual has the inclination towards drinking water but does not drink due to the fear of Allāh جل جلاله, hence the person is rewarded.

Qur'anic Wonders — Safety from Seduction

Within this verse, وَلَقَدْ هَمَّتْ بِهِ وَهَمَّ بِهَا, the word هَمَّ has been used twice. However, there is a difference between the هَمْ (thought) which Sayyidunā Yūsuf عليه السلام had and the هَمْ (thought) Zulaikha had. When stating the هَمْ (thought) which Zulaikha had, the letters لَامْ and قَدْ have been attached - these two letters display emphasis. However, there are no letters/emphasis present regarding the هَمْ (thought) Sayyidunā Yūsuf عليه السلام had. If there was no difference between the two thoughts, Allāh ﷻ could have said something similar to that of وَلَقَدْ هَمَّابِهِ. However, as Allāh ﷻ mentioned the two thoughts differently, this points towards the fact that there is a difference present between the two thoughts.

What are the signs/proofs that Allāh ﷻ gave to Sayyidunā Yūsuf عليه السلام?

1. The first proof/sign from Allāh ﷻ was that Sayyidunā Yūsuf عليه السلام thought, "How could I be so unfaithful to Allāh ﷻ after He has gifted me with a good residence?" (أَحْسَنَ مَثْوَايَ)

2. The second proof/sign from Allāh ﷻ was that Allāh ﷻ made Sayyidunā Ya'qūb عليه السلام appear in front of Sayyidunā Yūsuf عليه السلام. Sayyidunā Ya'qūb عليه السلام appeared with his finger within his mouth almost as a sign of showing regret. Upon seeing this situation of his father, Sayyidunā Yūsuf عليه السلام said he could not commit such an act.

3. Some Scholars of Tafsīr mention a third proof/sign from Allāh ﷻ which was that this verse was written upon the wall,

$$\text{وَلَا تَقْرَبُوا الزِّنَا إِنَّهُ كَانَ فَاحِشَةً}$$

"And do not even go close to fornication. Indeed it is an immoral act." (17:32)

Within the verse, لِنَصْرِفَ عَنْهُ السُّوءَ وَالْفَحْشَاءَ, the word اَلسُّوءَ refers to evil or it can refer to minor sins. The word اَلْفَحْشَاءَ refers to immorality or can refer to major sins.

There are two types of chosen people:

1. مُخْلَصٌ بِفَتْحِ اللَّامِ - This means Allāh ﷻ Himself has chosen an individual - this refers to all the Prophets عليهم السلام. They are free from sin before and after receiving Prophethood.

2. مُخْلِصٌ بِكَسْرِ اللَّامِ - This means that one works hard themselves to become a chosen servant of Allāh ﷻ.

<u>Lesson:</u> Whenever we get invited/inclined towards perpetrating any sort of evil acts, we should remember and always keep in mind the incident of Sayyidunā Yūsuf عليه السلام. We should seek refuge in Allāh ﷻ from committing such evil. We should all aspire to become مُخْلِص servants of Allāh ﷻ so that we attain His pleasure and mercy at all times.

Regret on Judgement Day

وَقَالَ الشَّيْطَانُ لَمَّا قُضِيَ الْأَمْرُ إِنَّ اللهَ وَعَدَكُمْ وَعْدَ الْحَقِّ وَوَعَدْتُكُمْ فَأَخْلَفْتُكُمْ وَمَا كَانَ لِيَ عَلَيْكُمْ مِّنْ سُلْطَانٍ إِلَّا أَنْ دَعَوْتُكُمْ فَاسْتَجَبْتُمْ لِي فَلَا تَلُومُونِي وَلُومُوا أَنْفُسَكُمْ مَا أَنَا بِمُصْرِخِكُمْ وَمَا أَنْتُمْ بِمُصْرِخِيَّ إِنِّي كَفَرْتُ بِمَا أَشْرَكْتُمُونِ مِنْ قَبْلُ إِنَّ الظَّالِمِينَ لَهُمْ عَذَابٌ أَلِيمٌ

"And Shaytān will say when the matter has been concluded: Indeed Allāh had promised you a truthful promise whilst I had promised you, but I betrayed you. I had no authority over you except that I invited you and you responded to me. So do not blame me; but blame yourselves. I cannot be of help to you and nor can you be of any help to me. Indeed I disown your associating me with Allāh in the past. Indeed for the wrongdoers is a painful punishment." (14:22)

This phrase لَمَّا قُضِيَ الْأَمْرُ refers to the time after the reckoning has taken place. Those who have been destined for Jannah will be escorted into Jannah and those who have been destined for Jahannam will be entered into Jahannam.

The inhabitants of Jahannam after entering will start to blame Shaytān, saying that it is his fault due to which they have entered into Jahannam.

They will ask his assistance and intercession in order to save themselves from the painful torment. In reply to their requests, Shaytān will reply,

$$إِنَّ اللّٰهَ وَعَدَكُمْ وَعْدَ الْحَقِّ وَوَعَدْتُكُمْ فَأَخْلَفْتُكُمْ$$

"Indeed Allāh had promised you a truthful promise whilst I had promised you, but I betrayed you." (14:22)

This aforementioned verse is the beginning of Shaytān's speech in front of the inhabitants of Jahannam.

Allāh ﷻ told mankind that they will be successful if they worship and fear Him. Allāh ﷻ through the means of sending many Prophets into this world, revealed the Holy Books which were a means of guidance for how we should live our daily lives.

The promise of Shaytān can be found in Sūrah An-Nisā,

$$وَلَأُضِلَّنَّهُمْ وَلَأُمَنِّيَنَّهُمْ وَلَآمُرَنَّهُمْ فَلَيُبَتِّكُنَّ اٰذَانَ الْأَنْعَامِ وَلَآمُرَنَّهُمْ فَلَيُغَيِّرُنَّ خَلْقَ اللّٰهِ$$

"And I will surely lead them astray and I will surely arouse them in sinful desires i.e. tempt them with false hopes. And I will surely command them so that they shall slit the ears of cattle and I will surely command them whereby they will change the creation of Allāh." (4:119)

Shaytān made a promise to Allāh ﷻ that he would surely misguide mankind and deceive them—Shaytān continuously gave hope to people by saying that there is no need to worship; a person is still young and has all the time left in their disposal to do these things later on!

Shaytān, on the Day of Judgement, will go against all his promises and free himself from blame. Shaytān will say, "Blame yourselves not me, as Allāh ﷻ did not leave you in the dark. For every era/Ummah (nation), Allāh ﷻ sent a guide which all humans had the free will to accept, thus I (Shaytān) cannot be blamed. I did not compel you to carry out anything; there is no use blaming each other now as we are all here together. The difference between us is that I took some enjoyment from the world from the era of Sayyidunā Ādam ﷷ until now."

Shaytān will tell his audience that there is no complete or strong evidence which can be presented. He (Shaytān) just adorned many things and showed them to us and we accepted his invitation.

In every era, there has always been a group of individuals who either worshipped idols, their own desires or the devil, hence Shaytān will say, "I do not accept anything," and will deny all these blames.

Lesson: We should aspire to constantly remain in the remembrance of Allāh ﷻ. This will save us from falling into the many traps of Shaytān. Let us all make firm intentions to follow Allāh's ﷻ commandments and the path of our Holy Prophet ﷺ in order for us to become successful in both worlds.

Enjoining Good & Forbidding Evil

$$\text{إِنَّ اللهَ يَأْمُرُ بِالْعَدْلِ وَالْإِحْسَانِ وَإِيتَاءِ ذِي الْقُرْبَىٰ وَيَنْهَىٰ عَنِ الْفَحْشَاءِ وَالْمُنْكَرِ وَالْبَغْيِ يَعِظُكُمْ لَعَلَّكُمْ تَذَكَّرُونَ}$$

"Indeed Allāh enjoins justice, adopting good behaviour and giving relatives (their due rights) and forbids shameful acts, evil deeds and oppression. He admonishes you so that you may be reminded." (16:90)

This verse is one of the most comprehensive verses within the Holy Qur'ān. Scholars say if there was no other verse revealed in terms of explanation then this verse would suffice. Sayyidunā Aktham ؓ and Sayyidunā Uthmān Ibn Madh'ūn ؓ both accepted Islām due to the comprehensiveness of this verse. Both leaders told their nations that this verse shows the Holy Prophet ﷺ enjoins good and forbids evil. If we deeply look into the verse, Allāh ﷻ makes mention of six things—three are pertaining to righteous actions (اَلْاَمْرُ) and three are pertaining to evil actions (اَلنَّهْيُ).

اَلْعَدْلُ refers to maintaining a high level of justice. Justice should be present within every aspect i.e. one should maintain moderation - one should not exceed or go below the limit.

Justice should be found within:
1. Beliefs عَقَائِدُ

2. Worship عِبَادَاتْ
3. Transactions مُعَامَلَاتْ
4. Societal affairs مُعَاشَرَاتْ
5. Conduct or morality اَخْلَاقْ

اَلْاِحْسَانْ means one should do good to others whether they are strangers, relatives, Muslim or non-Muslim. One should also encourage others to do the same. Within the Ahādīth of the Holy Prophet ﷺ, a famous Hadīth known as Hadīth Jibrīl, makes mention regarding the definition of Ihsān.

$$\text{أَنْ تَعْبُدَ اللّٰهَ كَأَنَّكَ تَرَاهُ فَإِنْ لَّمْ تَكُنْ تَرَاهُ فَإِنَّهُ يَرَاكَ}$$

"To worship Allāh as if you see Him, and if you do not see Him then truly He sees you." (Bukhārī, Muslim)

Ihsān here refers to obtaining the highest stage of worship/devotion. One should aspire to achieve this status and then motivate others towards attaining this also.

Even though the aforementioned acts include the relatives, Allāh ﷻ specifically mentioned this separately (وَإِيْتَاءِ ذِي الْقُرْبٰى) due to people generally overlooking this important matter i.e. treating relatives with kindness. This highlights the significance and importance of enjoining good with our relatives.

Sin and vice usually takes place due to three main factors which Allāh ﷻ is prohibiting in this verse:

1. قُوَّةُ الشَّهْوَانِيَّةِ (Carnal desires)
2. قُوَّةُ النَّفْسَانِيَّةِ (Selfish desires)
3. قُوَّةُ الْبَهِيمِيَّةِ (Animalistic traits)

1. اَلْفَحْشَاءُ (immorality) is committed due to قُوَّةُ الشَّهْوَانِيَّةِ (carnal desires).

2. اَلْمُنْكَرُ (sin) is the opposite of مَعْرُوْف (goodness). One commits sins due to قُوَّةُ النَّفْسَانِيَّةِ (selfish desires).

3. اَلْبَغْي means one exceeds the limit of oppression to such an extent where one loses self control over certain desires; this refers to قُوَّةُ الْبَهِيمِيَّةِ (Animalistic traits).

<u>Lesson:</u> Allāh ﷻ is reminding us all to eradicate all our evil traits and to inculcate all righteous traits- not just those mentioned within this verse but within the Holy Qur'ān as a whole. This will ultimately entail us to adopt humility and become obedient to Allāh ﷻ.

Upholding Promises

وَلَا تَكُونُوا كَالَّتِي نَقَضَتْ غَزْلَهَا مِنْ بَعْدِ قُوَّةٍ أَنْكَاثًا تَتَّخِذُونَ أَيْمَانَكُمْ دَخَلًا بَيْنَكُمْ أَنْ تَكُونَ أُمَّةٌ هِيَ أَرْبَىٰ مِنْ أُمَّةٍ إِنَّمَا يَبْلُوكُمُ اللَّهُ بِهِ وَلَيُبَيِّنَنَّ لَكُمْ يَوْمَ الْقِيَامَةِ مَا كُنْتُمْ فِيهِ تَخْتَلِفُونَ

"Do not be like the woman who had broken her yarn into pieces after spinning it firmly, by taking your oaths as means of deceit/mischief between yourselves, merely because one community is more plentiful (in number or wealth) than another community. Allāh thereby puts you to a test and He will surely make clear to you on the Day of Judgement all those matters in which you used to differ." (16:92)

This specific verse was revealed regarding a certain insane, old woman who resided within Makkah Mukarramah. She would weave from dawn till dusk and would reach the end stage whereby she had only to knot the item in order to finish it off.

However, upon reaching the end stage she would pull the thread, thereby undoing all the strands she had woven prior, and she would end up back to where she had started.

Allāh ﷻ is telling us in this verse not to make our pledges like the woman with her weaving. The pledge is so strong like the item which is woven, but we pull the thread so easily i.e. we break the promise so easily and the item/promise is left in ruins.

We break the pledge after it being so firm that it is as though we treat the matter lightly. Allāh ﷻ is telling us not to act so oblivious whilst fulfilling any covenant, peace treaty or agreement. We should not be under the impression that our promises are so trivial like a thread which has no real use, thus is very easy to break. Whenever we make a covenant or peace treaty whether it be with a Muslim, non-Muslim, group, organisation or country, we must fulfill it to the best of our ability.

This verse can also be applicable to how we treat our deeds. We try our best to gain a strong relationship with Allāh ﷻ within the month of Ramadhān by means of performing Tahajjud, recitation of the Holy Qur'ān and Dhikr etc. However, when the day of Eid arrives, everything ends, thus we undo the strong relationship we had tried so hard to obtain.

<u>Lesson:</u> We should continuously pray that Allāh ﷻ gives us the strength to perpetually worship Him and to not make us from amongst those who waste their effort, and treat their religion and deeds lightly and as of no consequence.

Kind Treatment to Parents

وَقَضَىٰ رَبُّكَ أَلَّا تَعْبُدُوا إِلَّا إِيَّاهُ وَبِالْوَالِدَيْنِ إِحْسَانًا إِمَّا يَبْلُغَنَّ عِندَكَ الْكِبَرَ أَحَدُهُمَا أَوْ كِلَاهُمَا فَلَا تَقُل لَّهُمَا أُفٍّ وَلَا تَنْهَرْهُمَا وَقُل لَّهُمَا قَوْلًا كَرِيمًا وَاخْفِضْ لَهُمَا جَنَاحَ الذُّلِّ مِنَ الرَّحْمَةِ وَقُل رَّبِّ ارْحَمْهُمَا كَمَا رَبَّيَانِي صَغِيرًا

"And your Lord has decreed that you worship none but Him and do good to parents. If any one of them or both of them reach old age, do not say to them Uff (a word or expression of anger/contempt) and do not scold them, but address them with respectful words and submit yourself before them in humility and out of compassion, and say, My Lord, be merciful to them as they have brought me up in my childhood." (17:23-24)

Allāh ﷻ, after His worship, mentions that the next most important thing is being kind towards our parents - not just the father or just the mother; rather both parents. The true reason for a person's existence is through Allāh's ﷻ grace. The apparent reason for a person's existence in the world is through their parents. The parents are the apparent means for an individual to enter into this world.

Within the Ahādīth of the Holy Prophet ﷺ, it states that the mother should be the one whom a person should spend more of their time with in terms of Khidmah (service).

This was mentioned three times by the Holy Prophet ﷺ followed by the father. The question could arise as to why the mother was mentioned three times. The answer is because a woman goes through three specific difficulties which is exclusive to her only.

1. During the time when the child is in the mother's womb.

2. During the time when the mother is giving birth. This is a very laborious time for the mother.

3. During the breastfeeding duration of two years.

After the initial two years have passed, the father commences his responsibility over the child as well as the mother.

Allāh ﷻ mentions in Sūrah Luqmān,

$$\text{وَوَصَّيْنَا الْإِنسَانَ بِوَالِدَيْهِ حَمَلَتْهُ أُمُّهُ وَهْنًا عَلَىٰ وَهْنٍ وَفِصَالُهُ فِي عَامَيْنِ أَنِ اشْكُرْ لِي وَلِوَالِدَيْكَ إِلَيَّ الْمَصِيرُ}$$

"And We have enjoined upon man (care) for his parents. His mother carried him (in her womb) despite weakness upon weakness, and his weaning is in two years. (We said to man,) 'Be grateful to Me and to your parents. To Me is the ultimate return.' (31:14)

From the beginning until the end of the pregnancy period, the mother undergoes so many hardships for the child. However, we do not value our parents - especially our mother who undertook many difficulties. Unfortunately, often the value of the mother is realised when it is too late. For example, a woman will appreciate the value of her mother when she has her own children; how much her own mother went through. Men will realise how many hardships their own mothers had to go through when they see their own wives going through the pregnancy period. Even if a parent oppresses their child, it is still necessary for the child to treat his/her parents with kindness.

Old age was mentioned because parents usually become very sensitive over petty things when they reach old age. A person will receive abundant amount of reward for tolerating the behaviour of their parents (during their old age).

The word أُفٍّ in the Arabic language is to show the lowest level of disrespect. The word أُفٍّ is a bad word itself, hence should be avoided.

Every couple should realize that even when there is an altercation between mother in-law and daughter in-law, the husband should always maintain the respect for his mother. This is because a mother is more sensitive in comparison to his wife. Even if the mother is wrong, disrespecting her is not permitted.

Mufti Shafī Sāhib ؒ mentions that in order to save the children from a major sin (disrespect of parents) the parents before commanding the children to do something, should say, "It would be good/nice if you could do this" and not say, "Do this". If a child does not carry out the order, then at least he will not be perpetrating a major sin even though this will be condemned as well.

In this era, it is common that many youth will answer back to their parents and think their parents are backwards and unmodernised. This is a very unpleasant conception and should be eradicated. This is a sign of pride that the child be under the impression they know more than their parents. Sa'eed Ibnul Mussayib ﷺ states that a person should talk to their parents in a similar manner to how a slave who ran away from the master would speak after they have been caught. The slave will appease the master by praising them.

Our Akābir (pious predecessors) had immense respect for their parents that they had more respect for their parents than their own teachers! Uwais Qarni ﷺ did not attain the status of a Sahābī for no other reason but due to attending to the Khidmah (service) of his mother.

<u>Lesson:</u> It is said that a mother can look after ten children, but ten children cannot look after one mother - this is the sad reality we face in this day and age. We need to make a firm resolution to always appreciate and look after our parents whilst they are still alive so that we do not regret afterwards. If they are not alive, we should pray this Du'ā for them after every Salāh: رَبِّ ارْحَمْهُمَا كَمَا رَبَّيَانِيْ صَغِيْرًا

How Many Youngsters?

سَيَقُوْلُوْنَ ثَلٰثَةٌ رَّابِعُهُمْ كَلْبُهُمْ وَيَقُوْلُوْنَ خَمْسَةٌ سَادِسُهُمْ كَلْبُهُمْ رَجْمًا بِالْغَيْبِ وَيَقُوْلُوْنَ سَبْعَةٌ وَّثَامِنُهُمْ كَلْبُهُمْ قُلْ رَّبِّيْ أَعْلَمُ بِعِدَّتِهِمْ مَّا يَعْلَمُهُمْ إِلَّا قَلِيْلٌ فَلَا تُمَارِ فِيْهِمْ إِلَّا مِرَاءً ظَاهِرًا وَّلَا تَسْتَفْتِ فِيْهِمْ مِّنْهُمْ أَحَدًا

"They will say there were three; the fourth of them being their dog and some will say there were five; the sixth being their dog – guessing at the unseen. And others will say there were seven and the eighth was their dog. Say (O Muhammad), 'My Lord knows best about their number. No one knows them except a few, so do not argue about them except with an obvious argument. And do not enquire about them from anyone among them (the speculators).'" (18:22)

سَيَقُوْلُوْنَ is referring to the polytheists of Makkah. They were debating regarding how many youngsters were actually present within the cave. The Holy Qur'ān is thus mentioning the different opinions they put forth.

Allāh ﷻ has brought the clause رَجْمًا بِالْغَيْبِ (guessing about the unseen) for those who opine there were three or five. This clause signifies doubt which shows that there were neither three & four or five & six. This doubtful opinion hence has no evidence to show it is correct.

For those who opine seven & eight, there are three pieces of evidence:

1. Allāh ﷻ has brought the letter وَاوْ for those who opine there were seven & eight. This وَاوْ generally comes to highlight emphasis and to explain something with clarity.

2. The second evidence is that after the word كَلْبُهُمْ, there is no clause of doubt (رَجْمًاۢ بِالْغَيْبِ) unlike the first two opinions (three/four or five/six).

There is a big difference between the two opinions. Those who opine three/four or five/six were merely estimates. There were three; the dog is the fourth or there were five; the sixth is the dog. However, those who opine seven, Allāh ﷻ puts forward the letter وَاوْ there were seven <u>and</u> the dog is the eighth.

Allāh ﷻ is best aware with regards to the actual number of youth in the cave.

3. With regards to this verse, Sayyidunā Abdullāh Ibn Abbās ؓ, the leader of all the Mufassirūn says,

اَنَا قَلِيْلٌ مِّنْهُمْ

"I am from amongst the few (who possess knowledge with regards to the amount) and it is my opinion that there were seven youngsters."

His statement thus suffices as the third piece of evidence. If we look towards a previous verse,

$$وَكَذَٰلِكَ بَعَثْنَاهُمْ لِيَتَسَاءَلُوا بَيْنَهُمْ قَالَ قَائِلٌ مِّنْهُمْ كَمْ لَبِثْتُمْ قَالُوا لَبِثْنَا يَوْمًا أَوْ بَعْضَ يَوْمٍ قَالُوا رَبُّكُمْ أَعْلَمُ بِمَا لَبِثْتُمْ$$

"And similarly, We awakened them so they might question one another. A speaker said from among them, 'How long have you remained (here)?' They said, 'We have remained a day or part of a day.' They said, 'Your Lord is most knowing of how long you remained.'" (18:19)

We come to realise from this verse that there were seven youngsters all together, hence another supporting evidence. This verse is regarding the conversation between the different youngsters of the cave.

1. قَالَ قَائِلٌ مِّنْهُمْ – This firstly proves there is <u>one</u> individual so far.
2. قَالُوا لَبِثْنَا يَوْمًا أَوْ بَعْضَ يَوْمٍ – This secondly proves there are another <u>three</u> individuals as the least number قَالُوا can refer to is three.
3. قَالُوا رَبُّكُمْ أَعْلَمُ بِمَا لَبِثْتُمْ - This in addition proves there are another <u>three</u> individuals as the least number قَالُوا can refer to is three.

Therefore, there were seven youngsters in total in the cave.

وَاللّٰهُ أَعْلَمُ (Only Allāh ﷺ knows best).

Etiquettes of Supplication

$$\text{كهيعص ذِكْرُ رَحْمَةِ رَبِّكَ عَبْدَهُ زَكَرِيَّا إِذْ نَادَىٰ رَبَّهُ نِدَاءً خَفِيًّا قَالَ رَبِّ إِنِّي وَهَنَ الْعَظْمُ مِنِّي وَاشْتَعَلَ الرَّأْسُ شَيْبًا وَلَمْ أَكُن بِدُعَائِكَ رَبِّ شَقِيًّا وَإِنِّي خِفْتُ الْمَوَالِيَ مِن وَرَائِي وَكَانَتِ امْرَأَتِي عَاقِرًا فَهَبْ لِي مِن لَّدُنكَ وَلِيًّا يَرِثُنِي وَيَرِثُ مِنْ آلِ يَعْقُوبَ ۖ وَاجْعَلْهُ رَبِّ رَضِيًّا}$$

"(This is) a mention of the mercy of your Lord upon His servant Zakariyyā, when he called his Lord in a low voice. He said, 'My Lord, indeed my bones have weakened, and my head is filled with white hair and never have I remained in my supplication to You, my Lord, unanswered. And indeed, I fear my kinsmen after me and my wife is barren, so bless me with an heir from Yourself who will inherit me and inherit from the family of Ya'qūb. And make him, my Lord, pleasing (to You).'" (19:1-6)

Allāh ﷻ bestowed two exclusive types of mercy upon Sayyidunā Zakariyyā عليه السلام:
1. Prophethood.
2. A child in his old age.

Many Scholars are of the opinion that in general cases, to perform Du'ā secretly/softly is most preferable. The reason is because one will perform the supplication with sincerity and is able to have a close and personal relationship with Allāh ﷻ. However, whilst sitting within large gatherings, it is best to perform Du'ā collectively and audibly as all the participants can say Āmīn after the Du'ā, so that it be accepted.

The question could arise as to what the need was for Sayyidunā Zakariyyā ﷺ to perform Du'ā secretly? The answer is that if Sayyidunā Zakariyyā ﷺ performed Du'ā in front of everyone, they would mock and laugh at him saying, "Look at this old man who is beseeching Allāh ﷻ for a child in his old age!" This demonstrates the amazing wisdom of Sayyidunā Zakariyyā ﷺ. For example, if one supplicates to Allāh ﷻ in front of a large audience to become a millionaire, people may believe that this person is very greedy for money - even though there is no harm in asking for such Du'ās, but certain Du'ās should be done discreetly.

The more one humbles oneself in front of Allāh ﷻ, the more Allāh ﷻ loves that supplication which has a large effect and impact; in attracting the mercy of Allāh ﷻ.

وَلَمْ أَكُنۢ بِدُعَآئِكَ رَبِّ شَقِيًّا - When one is in the presence of a king and one says to the king, "Whenever I asked anything from yourself, you never deprived me or rejected me; you gave me more than I asked." The king upon hearing this, will become very happy and will realise that this individual is very appreciative, hence the king will feel like granting more to the person.

In the same way, Sayyidunā Zakariyyā ﷺ is proclaiming to Allāh ﷻ that O Allāh ﷻ, whenever I pleaded for anything from You, You never rejected my supplication and never deprived me; You gave me more than I asked for. Allāh ﷻ will want to give more to His servants if they are appreciative of His blessings.

This is all in the introduction - Sayyidunā Zakariyyā ؑ has not at this point, even asked for a child yet. He is bringing all this forward to attract the mercy of Allāh ﷻ.

وَاجْعَلْهُ رَبِّ رَضِيًّا - This is the ultimate thing we should plead for. When we ask for a child, don't just ask for a boy or a girl - rather we should ask Allāh ﷻ to make the child His beloved and to make the child obedient, and upon whom He is pleased with. This teaches us that whenever we ask Allāh ﷻ for anything, we should ask for the best e.g. we should not just ask Allāh ﷻ to enter us into Jannah (Paradise); rather enter us into Jannatul Firdaus (the highest place in Paradise).

<u>Lesson:</u> Whenever we make Du'ā to Allāh ﷻ, we should adopt these certain methods and etiquettes and keep them in mind thinking, "O Allāh ﷻ, you gave me everything I asked for and those things which I did not even ask for; O Allāh ﷻ, You can give me more and grant me the best."

Absence of Tears

$$\text{أُولَٰئِكَ الَّذِينَ أَنْعَمَ اللَّهُ عَلَيْهِمْ مِنَ النَّبِيِّينَ مِنْ ذُرِّيَّةِ آدَمَ وَمِمَّنْ حَمَلْنَا مَعَ نُوحٍ وَمِنْ ذُرِّيَّةِ إِبْرَاهِيمَ وَإِسْرَائِيلَ وَمِمَّنْ هَدَيْنَا وَاجْتَبَيْنَا إِذَا تُتْلَىٰ عَلَيْهِمْ آيَاتُ الرَّحْمَٰنِ خَرُّوا سُجَّدًا وَبُكِيًّا}$$

"These are the people whom Allāh has blessed with bounties from amongst the Prophets, from the progeny of Ādam and of those whom We caused to board (the ark) along with Nūh and from the progeny of Ibrāhīm and Isrā'īl and from those whom We guided and choose. When the verses of the All-Merciful are recited before them, they fall in prostration while they are weeping." (19:58)

إِذَا تُتْلَىٰ عَلَيْهِمْ آيَاتُ الرَّحْمَٰنِ خَرُّوا سُجَّدًا وَبُكِيًّا - In this specific verse, two main traits have been mentioned. One is of prostrating and the second is of weeping. Upon this particular verse, Sayyidunā Umar ؓ used to say,

هٰذِهِ السَّجْدَةُ وَأَيْنَ الْبُكَاءُ؟

"I have performed the Sajdah (prostration), but where have my tears gone?"

It is said regarding Sayyidunā Umar ؓ that he would pray long Sūrahs during Fajr Salāh e.g. Sūrah Yūsuf and Sūrah Ra'd. He would cry profusely to such an extent, the Companions ؓ say,

كُنَّا نَسْمَعُ نَسِيْجَ عُمَرَ

"We would continuously hear the audible crying of Sayyidunā Umar ﷺ."

نَسِيْجَ is the sound one makes when one reaches the highest level of crying; a stage where they are unable to speak or pronounce words.

The Muhaddithūn (Scholars of Hadīth) mention if one is unable to cry, then one should impersonate/make the face of a crying person. This trait of being able to cry has been given such high importance that in all matters, we have not been given the command to impersonate; only when crying. It is said within the Ahādīth of the Holy Prophet ﷺ that those eyes which produce tears due to the fear of Allāh ﷻ will never touch the fire of Jahannam.

<u>Lesson:</u> In this day and age, we find it extremely difficult to cry - this trait has almost become scarce and bizarre to us when it comes to religious matters. We should pray to Allāh ﷻ to bestow us with the ability to gain a strong relationship with the Holy Qur'ān which will then allow us to instill this humble quality of shedding tears.

Different Levels of Salāh

فَخَلَفَ مِنْ بَعْدِهِمْ خَلْفٌ أَضَاعُوا الصَّلٰوةَ وَاتَّبَعُوا الشَّهَوٰتِ فَسَوْفَ يَلْقَوْنَ غَيًّا

"Then came after them the successors who neglected Salāh and pursued (their selfish) desires; so they will soon face (the outcome of their) deviation." (19:59)

Allāh ﷻ, after mentioning the qualities of the righteous, now mentions regarding the qualities of the disobedient.

There are four words which we must note in our minds:

خَلْف بِسُكُوْنِ اللَّام—(a bad forerunner)

سَلْف بِسُكُوْنِ اللَّام—(a bad predecessor)

خَلَف بِفَتْحِ اللَّام—(a pious forerunner)

سَلَف بِفَتْحِ اللَّام—(a pious predecessor)

The question could arise as to what makes a person woeful. The answer is mentioned within the verse - neglecting and destroying Salāh. Many Ulama have mentioned different stages of أَضَاعُوا الصَّلَاةَ

- مُنْكِرُ الصَّلٰوة - To become neglectful of Salāh means that one completely refuses to believe in the obligation of Salāh; these people are the disbelievers.

- تَارِكُ الصَّلٰوة—To become neglectful of performing Salāh means one accepts the obligation, but refuses to carry it out.

To become neglectful of performing Salāh means one performs the Salāh but in a careless manner. In the Hadīth, it mentions that this type of Salāh will be thrown back onto the face of that individual. To become neglectful of performing Salāh also means one does not perform their Salāh with the congregation i.e. with the Jamā'ah (for a man).

The word غَيًّا has two meanings. Firstly, it is another name for Hell. Some say غَيًّا is the name of a river in Hell. Secondly, it refers to misguidance.

<u>Lesson</u>: We seek the glitter of this world which is artificial and take the performance of Salāh so lightly and to be of little importance. The majority of us have become from the خَلْف (may Allāh ﷻ forgive us!). This verse is directly talking about us and our current situation. We need to amend our conduct and perform all of our Qadhā Umri (missed Salāh) in order to become successful in the Ākhirah (Hereafter).

The Successful Believers

قَدْ أَفْلَحَ الْمُؤْمِنُونَ الَّذِينَ هُمْ فِي صَلَاتِهِمْ خَاشِعُونَ وَالَّذِينَ هُمْ عَنِ اللَّغْوِ مُعْرِضُونَ وَالَّذِينَ هُمْ لِلزَّكَاةِ فَاعِلُونَ وَالَّذِينَ هُمْ لِفُرُوجِهِمْ حَافِظُونَ إِلَّا عَلَىٰ أَزْوَاجِهِمْ أَوْ مَا مَلَكَتْ أَيْمَانُهُمْ فَإِنَّهُمْ غَيْرُ مَلُومِينَ فَمَنِ ابْتَغَىٰ وَرَاءَ ذَٰلِكَ فَأُولَٰئِكَ هُمُ الْعَادُونَ وَالَّذِينَ هُمْ لِأَمَانَاتِهِمْ وَعَهْدِهِمْ رَاعُونَ وَالَّذِينَ هُمْ عَلَىٰ صَلَوَاتِهِمْ يُحَافِظُونَ

"Certainly, success is really attained by those believers who, when offering Salāh (prayers), concentrate their attention in humbleness and who turn/keep themselves away from ill speech/vain things and those who are performers of Zakāh and those who guard their private parts, except from their wives or from those (bondwomen who are) owned by their hands, as they are not to be blamed. However, those who seek (sexual pleasure) beyond that are the transgressors. And (success is attained) by those who are observers of their trusts and covenants. And those who carefully maintain their prayers." (23:1-9)

The first quality mentioned of the Believers is that of concentrating when offering Salāh (prayer). In the verse, the word خَاشِعُونَ means سَاكِتُونَ (those who are fixated in their Salāh i.e. they do not move at all and are completely focused).

The different stages of concentration

1. The first stage is Fardh. When raising the hands for Takbīr Tahrīmah (the opening Takbīr), one is aware regarding which Salāh they are offering.
2. The second stage is Wājib. Throughout the Salāh, a person is aware regarding the different postures i.e. standing (Qiyām), bowing and prostrating (Rukū & Sajdah) etc.
3. The third stage is Mustahab- this is the highest stage. Throughout the performance of Salāh, from the beginning to the end, a person is fully focused. In the Hadīth Jibrīl, Sayyidunā Jibrīl عليه السلام asked the Holy Prophet ﷺ regarding the meaning of Ihsān. The Holy Prophet ﷺ replied,

أَنْ تَعْبُدَ اللَّهَ كَأَنَّكَ تَرَاهُ فَإِنْ لَّمْ تَكُنْ تَرَاهُ فَإِنَّهُ يَرَاكَ

"That you worship Allāh as though you can see Allāh. If you cannot see Him, then remember that Allāh can see you." (Bukhāri, Muslim)

Ways to achieve the highest level of concentration

Hakīmul Ummah, Shaykh Ashraf Ali Thānwi ﷺ has given a remedy for attaining the Mustahab (highest) stage of concentration in Salāh.

He says one should perform their Salāh as if they are a 'Kacha Hāfiz' - a memoriser of the Holy Qur'ān who does not know their Qur'ān properly. This is because in Salāh whilst reciting the Qur'ān, the (weak) Hāfiz will have full concentration on every word and verse they are reading. So in the same way, a person who is not a Hāfiz should always be thinking about what they are reading whilst performing their Salāh.

Shaykh Muhammad Zakariyyā ﷺ states in order to reach the highest level of concentration, a person should perform their Salāh as if they are a slave who has run away from their master, and now the master has caught the slave. The servant will praise the master first as they know the master is angry. In the same way, before offering Salāh, Allāh ﷻ is angry with us due to us committing so many sins and having transgressed all the limits thus whilst standing, we start off by praising Him.

After this, if there is no response, the servant will bow/put the head down in full submission, praising and thanking the master for not executing him. Similarly, whilst in the posture of Rukū' (bowing), we praise Allāh ﷻ because He has not taken our lives away. After bowing the head, the servant will prostrate to his master and fall before the feet of the master for letting him remain alive. In the same manner, when we go into Sajdah (prostration), we fall in front of Allāh ﷻ showing gratitude towards Him as He has not taken our lives away due to our sins.

The second quality mentioned of the believers is of keeping oneself away from vain pursuits.

One should not interfere in anything which has got nothing to do with the person and is of no concern to them. لَغْوٌ (futile talk) can be with regards to talk, action or intention which is vain and has no benefit- neither worldly or in the Hereafter. If something is necessary then we should talk, otherwise we should keep silent.

In the Holy Qur'ān, whilst mentioning the qualities of the servants of the Rahmān (the All-Merciful), Allāh ﷻ states,

وَالَّذِيْنَ لَا يَشْهَدُوْنَ الزُّوْرَ وَإِذَا مَرُّوْا بِاللَّغْوِ مَرُّوْا كِرَامًا

"And (the servants of Allāh are) those who do not testify to falsehood. When they pass by any futile things, they pass in an honourable way." (25:72)

When a person passes by something which is wrong, they should lower their gaze and hasten their pace in order to move away. If there is some wrong taking place, an individual should not look at it and instead should move away.

The Holy Prophet ﷺ said,

مِنْ حُسْنِ إِسْلَامِ الْمَرْءِ تَرْكُهُ مَا لَا يَعْنِيْهِ

"From a person's goodness of Islām is that he leaves that which does not concern him." (Tirmizi)

This Ḥadīth has the value of 100,000 Aḥādīth according to Imām Abū Dāwūd ﷺ! From the 500,000 Aḥādīth which Imām Abū Dāwūd ﷺ knew and collected, this Ḥadīth, along with three others, he categorised as the foundation of Islām.

The second Ḥadīth is,

$$\text{إِنَّمَا الْأَعْمَالُ بِالنِّيَّاتِ}$$

"Actions are according to intentions." (Bukhārī, Muslim)

The third Ḥadīth is,

$$\text{لَا يُؤْمِنُ أَحَدُكُمْ حَتَّى يُحِبَّ لِأَخِيهِ مَا يُحِبُّ لِنَفْسِه}$$

"None of you will truly become believers until you love for your brother what you love for yourself." (Bukhārī, Muslim)

The fourth Ḥadīth is,

$$\text{اَلْحَلَالُ بَيِّنٌ وَالْحَرَامُ بَيِّنٌ وَبَيْنَهُمَا أُمُورٌ مُشْتَبِهَاتٌ}$$

"Lawful is clear and unlawful is clear. And in between are doubtful matters." (Bukhārī, Muslim)

Imām Abu Ḥanīfah ﷺ has included another Ḥadīth,

$$\text{اَلْمُسْلِمُ مَنْ سَلِمَ الْمُسْلِمُونَ مِنْ لِسَانِه وَيَدِهِ}$$

"A Muslim is the one from whose tongue and hands another Muslim is safe." (Bukhāri)

The third quality mentioned of the believers is of those who discharge Zakāh (charity). Allāh ﷻ did not mention, وَالَّذِيْنَ هُمْ يُؤَدُّوْنَ الزَّكُوٰةَ (those who fulfill/pay Zakāh). Instead Allāh ﷻ used the word فَاعِلُوْنَ which gives the meaning of continuity - a person always gives Zakāh; not only in the month of Ramadhān, but throughout the entire year.

Usually, we tend to only think about giving Zakāh in the month of Ramadhān and for the rest of the eleven months, we don't focus towards caring for the poor and tend to neglect them. Zakāh and Sadaqah should continuously be given. Allāh ﷻ has made giving Zakāh very easy; the more the effort, the less one has to give.

Under the verse,

وَآتُوْا حَقَّهُ يَوْمَ حَصَادِهٖ

"And pay its due (Zakāh) on the day of harvest." (6:141)

Scholars of Tafsīr mention there are different categories of "Pay its due on the day of harvest". For example, if a person purchases a house and enters into its cellar and finds a huge treasure, or if a person purchased a piece of land and started digging to cultivate the crops and suddenly finds a huge treasure, then the ruling is they give 20% of that treasure to the poor. The Sharīah (Islamic law) is saying that a person can have this 80% - only one fifth will go to the poor.

Similarly, if a person has a piece of land, cultivated it through the natural way (through the rain and the sun), in this situation 10% is given. The reason is because slightly more effort has been carried out in this process. If a person used their own cattle and own equipment, in that situation 5% is given to the poor. The business profit where a person has worked all year through, only 2.5% is given to the poor. Therefore, the harder a person works, the less they give to the needy.

Umar Ibn Abdul Azīz ﷺ remained the Caliph for only two years. However, in them two years there was a tremendous transformation. It is mentioned that during his Caliphate, a time came that there was not a single person left eligible for Zakāh as everyone had ample provision. He continued implementing the Islamic system, hence the rich gave their Zakāh to the poor to the extent that the poor had enough surplus amounts so they could not take any more Zakāh money; how efficient the Islamic system is!

In Islām, the wealth doesn't only remain with the wealthy, it rotates. Unfortunately, now the system is such that the rich get richer and the poor get poorer.

The fourth quality mentioned of the believers is of those who guard their private parts and chastity— this includes both males and females. They do not fall into adultery, fornication and all other sinful acts. Instead, they fulfill their desires in the Halāl (lawful) way by means of marriage.

Allāh ﷻ has given us the lawful and unlawful system which are both presented in front of us. The lawful system is to fulfil one's desires by marriage and the unlawful system is to fulfil one's desires outside of marriage. Unfortunately, because recognition of the importance of marriage is diminishing, the unlawful system has become rampant within our society. The choice is ours to select which system we will follow. Allāh ﷻ has given humans intellect to distinguish between right and wrong.

فَمَنِ ابْتَغَىٰ وَرَاءَ ذَٰلِكَ فَأُولَٰئِكَ هُمُ الْعَادُونَ

"However, those who seek (sexual pleasure) beyond that are the transgressors." (23:7)

The Scholars of Tafsīr state that this verse refers to fulfilling the desires through dating, homosexuality, masturbation, fornication, adultery etc. There is a difference between fornication and adultery. Fornication refers to an unmarried couple engaging in any unlawful relationship. Adultery refers to any married individual engaging in an extra marital affair.

In this verse, Mut'ah is also included: fixing a marriage for a stipulated amount of time. For example, getting a marriage contract for only one month. To fulfill one's desires through these means is Harām (prohibited). If a person seeks another way other than the lawful way, they will be transgressing the limits.

Important Point: Imām Ālūsī ﷺ under the commentary of this

verse, in his Kitāb, Rūhul Ma'āni states that this refers to اِسْتِعْمَالُ الْيَدِ (Masturbation). Masturbation for a male and a female is completely Harām (prohibited) in Islām.

Allāh ﷻ mentions in Sūrah Nūr,

وَأَنكِحُوا الْأَيَامَى مِنكُمْ وَالصَّالِحِينَ مِنْ عِبَادِكُمْ وَإِمَائِكُمْ إِن يَكُونُوا فُقَرَاءَ يُغْنِهِمُ اللَّهُ مِن فَضْلِهِ وَاللَّهُ وَاسِعٌ عَلِيمٌ

"Arrange the marriage of the spouseless among you, and the capable from among your bondmen and bondwomen. If they are poor, Allāh will enrich them out of His grace. Allāh is All-Encompassing, All-Knowing." (24:32)

If a person becomes Bāligh (mature), does not get married and commits sins i.e. fulfills their desires in an unlawful manner, they will be sinful as well as the parents. Therefore marriage should take place as soon as possible in order to safeguard and preserve the chastity of an individual. Marriage becomes compulsory when a person fears or knows they will fall into sin.

The Holy Prophet ﷺ once mentioned,

يَا مَعْشَرَ الشَّبَابِ مَنِ اسْتَطَاعَ مِنْكُمُ الْبَاءَةَ فَلْيَنْكِحْ فَإِنَّهُ أَغَضُّ لِلْبَصَرِ وَأَحْصَنُ لِلْفَرْجِ وَمَنْ لَمْ يَسْتَطِعْ فَعَلَيْهِ بِالصَّوْمِ فَإِنَّهُ لَهُ وِجَاءٌ

"O young men, whoever amongst you have the ability to get married, let him get married for it is more effective in lowering the gaze and guarding chastity. Whoever cannot (afford to) get married, let him fast for that will be a shield for him." (Bukhāri, Muslim)

When the Holy Prophet ﷺ mentioned, "The ability to get married" it means physically and financially.

The fifth quality mentioned of the believers is of those who honestly look after their trusts and covenants. This refers to any financial trust or verbal promise in a person's life. For example, if a person tells their friend to meet them at a specific time and they do not show up on time, this is against the trust and becomes a sin.

If someone signs an application form in order to enroll themselves into an institution and on the form it states, "I will fully abide by all the rules and regulations of the institution," this is a promise. If the institution starts at five o'clock and the person arrives at half past five or comes late, this is a form of breaching the promise.

In the UK, we have certain laws whilst driving on the roads. When a person has passed their driving test and is living in this country, they have promised that they will abide by all the rules and regulations. For example, when driving on the motorway, a person cannot drive more than seventy miles per hour, thus if one does go over the speed limit of seventy miles per hour, a person will be breaking the law. A person will be sinful in the eyes of Allāh ﷻ and guilty in the sight of the government as well.

The biggest promise is the promise which Allāh ﷻ took in Ālam Arwāh (world of souls),

$$\text{أَلَسْتُ بِرَبِّكُمْ قَالُوا بَلَىٰ}$$

"Am I not Your Lord? They replied, 'Indeed You are.'" (7:172)

This was a promise we humans made to Allāh ﷻ, hence we must fulfill this promise by worshipping Allāh ﷻ in the correct manner.

The Islamic system is based on fixed times, for example the five daily prayers. In Sūrah Nisā, Allāh ﷻ states,

$$\text{إِنَّ الصَّلٰوةَ كَانَتْ عَلَى الْمُؤْمِنِينَ كِتَابًا مَوْقُوتًا}$$

"Surely, Salāh (prayer) is an obligation upon the believers that is stipulated on fixed times." (4:103)

Therefore a person cannot say, "I will work a twelve hour shift and at the end pray all the five daily prayers." When any promise is made, a person has to fulfil the promise, otherwise this will be a sign of hypocrisy. In a Hadīth it states,

$$\text{آيَةُ الْمُنَافِقِ ثَلَاثٌ إِذَا حَدَّثَ كَذَبَ وَإِذَا وَعَدَ أَخْلَفَ وَإِذَا اؤْتُمِنَ خَانَ}$$

"The signs of a hypocrite are three: when he speaks he lies, when he makes a promise he breaks it, and when he is trusted he goes against that trust." (Bukhārī, Muslim)

It is mentioned within the books of Sīrah (biography of the Holy Prophet ﷺ) that even before his Prophethood, the Holy Prophet ﷺ kept his promises. Once, the Holy Prophet's ﷺ friend, Abdullāh agreed to a business transaction with the Holy Prophet ﷺ. Abdullāh said, "I am coming, just wait here." He then went away and may have forgotten, but the Holy Prophet ﷺ remained standing there because he told him to wait. After three days, Abdullāh was passing by that road and saw the Holy Prophet ﷺ and said, "You are still standing here?" The Holy Prophet ﷺ replied, "I have been standing here for the last three days." Subhān-Allāh! Nowadays we could not even conceive such a thing.

Amīrul Muminīn (Leader of the believers), Sayyidunā Umar ؓ says, "Before you wish to say anything good about a person, ensure you either do a transaction with that person or you travel with them."

Whilst doing a transaction, a person will be able to see how trustworthy a person is and whether or not they have the fear of Allāh ﷻ within them. The Arabic word سَفَر means to illuminate. This means a person's character will become illuminated whilst traveling e.g. a person's bad habits will show and become apparent during this time.

The sixth quality mentioned of the believers is of those who carefully maintain their prayers. In this verse, the word يُحَافِظُونَ is mentioned in the present/future tense. This means a person is performing their Salāh properly, in the correct manner, now and will continue to do so in the future. The scale used is مُفَاعَلَة which is used to indicate the action from both sides—if a person carefully maintains their prayers, their Salāh will maintain them. The Holy Prophet ﷺ said,

$$\text{مَنْ صَلَّى صَلَاةَ الصُّبْحِ فَهُوَ فِي ذِمَّةِ اللهِ}$$

"A person who prays their Fajr (morning) prayer is under the protection of Allāh ﷻ." (Muslim)

In the Holy Qur'ān, Allāh ﷻ mentions,

$$\text{إِنَّ الصَّلٰوةَ تَنْهٰى عَنِ الْفَحْشَاءِ وَالْمُنْكَرِ}$$

"Indeed Salāh restrains an individual from committing shameful and evil acts." (29:45)

It is mentioned regarding the Holy Prophet ﷺ, that whenever something would concern or worry him, he would hasten towards performing Salāh.

In another verse, Allāh ﷻ mentions,

$$\text{وَاسْتَعِينُوْا بِالصَّبْرِ وَالصَّلٰوةِ وَإِنَّهَا لَكَبِيْرَةٌ إِلَّا عَلَى الْخٰشِعِيْنَ}$$

"Seek assistance through patience and prayer. It is indeed difficult except for the one who is humbly submissive to Allāh." (2:45)

أُولَٰئِكَ هُمُ الْوَارِثُونَ "Those are the inheritors" i.e. of Jannah (Paradise).

The word اَلْوَارِثُونَ is used because when a person receives inheritance, it can never be taken away from him because it is ordained from Allāh ﷻ. The word اَلْوَارِثُونَ gives the meaning of continuity, hence those destined for Jannah (Paradise), will remain forever in Jannah (Paradise). Once a person possesses all the above mentioned qualities within them and receives Jannah (Paradise), it will never be taken away from them.

The first quality started with Salāh and the last quality is also about Salāh; this signifies the importance of this act of worship - the distinguishing factor between Imān (belief) and Kufr (disbelief) is Salāh. If a person neglects their Salāh, they will fall into the ditch of Kufr (disbelief).

In the Holy Qur'ān, it is mentioned that the dwellers of Jannah (Paradise) will say to the dwellers of Jahannam (Hell),

مَا سَلَكَكُمْ فِي سَقَرَ قَالُوا لَمْ نَكُ مِنَ الْمُصَلِّينَ

"What has brought you to Saqar? (Hell). They (the dwellers of Hell) will say, we were not among those who offered Salāh (obligatory prayer)." (74:42-43)

This verse explains that a person, even though is a believer, can end up in Jahannam due to not performing Salāh. May Allāh ﷻ save us all! Āmīn.

Lesson: These verses explain the qualities of the true believers who will be successful on the Day of Judgement and in this world. We must earnestly reflect over these qualities mentioned by Allāh ﷻ and try our utmost to inculcate them into our daily lives. This world is the place where we should be engrossed in performing good deeds. Once a person fulfils this main goal (of worship), the only thing awaiting for that person is Jannah (Paradise), which will be eternal.

How Long Did We Live For?

Allāh ﷻ has given us life and time in this world to prepare for our eternal life in the Hereafter. When we will face Allāh ﷻ on the Day of Judgement, Allāh ﷻ is going to address and question every single one of us with one particular question,

كَمْ لَبِثْتُمْ فِي الْأَرْضِ عَدَدَ سِنِينَ

"How long did you live for whilst on this earth?" (23:112)

The creation will start to contemplate and try to recall how long they lived and in the Qur'ān, Allāh ﷻ mentions in various verses the different answers and replies people will be giving.

In one verse, Allāh ﷻ says,

يَتَخَافَتُونَ بَيْنَهُمْ إِنْ لَبِثْتُمْ إِلَّا عَشْرًا

"They will be whispering amongst themselves, 'You remained ten days in the world.'" (20:103)

Another group of people who will be more sensible and intelligent will reply that duration in this world for ten days was too much.

نَحْنُ أَعْلَمُ بِمَا يَقُولُونَ إِذْ يَقُولُ أَمْثَلُهُمْ طَرِيقَةً إِنْ لَبِثْتُمْ إِلَّا يَوْمًا

> "We know very well what they say, when the best of them in manner will say, 'You did not remain more than one day.'" (20:104)

In Sūrah Nāziāt, Allāh ﷻ states another group's response will be that one day is too much,

$$كَأَنَّهُمْ يَوْمَ يَرَوْنَهَا لَمْ يَلْبَثُوٓا۟ إِلَّا عَشِيَّةً أَوْ ضُحَىٰهَا$$

"It will seem to them as if they did not live in the world except for an evening or a morning." (79:46)

When the Day of Judgement will take place, some will say,

$$وَيَوْمَ تَقُومُ السَّاعَةُ يُقْسِمُ ٱلْمُجْرِمُونَ مَا لَبِثُوا۟ غَيْرَ سَاعَةٍ كَذَٰلِكَ كَانُوا۟ يُؤْفَكُونَ$$

"And on the Day when the Hour will take place, the criminals/sinners will swear that they had remained for only an hour. Thus, they were deluded." (30:55)

The Scholars of Tafsīr mention سَاعَةٌ refers to a very little amount of time; a split second. The diacritical point comes to give emphasis of تَقْلِيْل (a small amount).

After presenting all these differing replies, the creation will finally try to come to a conclusion.

$$\text{قَالُوا لَبِثْنَا يَوْمًا أَوْ بَعْضَ يَوْمٍ}$$

"They will say, 'We lived for a day or part of a day.'" (23:113)

Whatever the amount is, we do not know. In order to know the correct amount, who should we ask?

$$\text{فَسْأَلِ الْعَادِّينَ}$$

"Ask those who have been counting (referring to the Angels)." (23:113)

The Angels have been recording and noting down everything that we have done, so ask them. They will say,

$$\text{إِن لَّبِثْتُمْ إِلَّا قَلِيلًا ۖ لَّوْ أَنَّكُمْ كُنتُمْ تَعْلَمُونَ}$$

"You only lived for a small amount of time, only if you knew (how to value this time)." (23:114)

<u>Lesson:</u> After pondering over this incident, we should remind ourselves that we must not waste this short period of time we possess and should value every moment wisely. Yesterday was history, tomorrow is a mystery and today is a present; a gift. We need to utilise this gift. Whenever we get the opportunity of carrying out something good we should do it immediately and wholeheartedly.

Modesty

$$\text{قُلْ لِلْمُؤْمِنِيْنَ يَغُضُّوْا مِنْ أَبْصَارِهِمْ وَيَحْفَظُوْا فُرُوْجَهُمْ ذٰلِكَ أَزْكٰى لَهُمْ إِنَّ اللهَ خَبِيْرٌۢ بِمَا يَصْنَعُوْنَ}$$

"Say (O' Muhammad) to the believing men that they must lower their gazes and guard their private parts; that is more purer for them. Surely Allāh is All-Knowing of what they do." (24:30)

The question could arise as to why Allāh ﷻ gave the command to the Holy Prophet ﷺ of informing the men to lower their gazes and guard their private parts and not directly say it Himself?

This can be understood through an example of a father and son's relationship. Sometimes between a father and son, there are those things which are sensitive to discuss. Therefore, the father will tell a person who is close to the son e.g. an elder brother or a friend to inform the son of the matter. In the same manner, Allāh ﷻ says this is a delicate thing to discuss, thus out of modesty, Allāh ﷻ gave the command to the one close to the Companions ؓ i.e. the Holy Prophet ﷺ.

The word مِنْ here gives the meaning of تَبْعِيْض (partiality). This means that the believing men do not have to lower their gazes from everything; only during specific situations.

There are two main instances in which a man should lower his gaze.

1. Any unknown woman (Ghair Mahram woman) with a lustful intent.
2. To look at any individual with the intention of belittling them.

Apart from these two instances, it is permissible for a man not to lower his gaze e.g. whilst in the presence of his parents.

The Aḥādīth mentions that if an unintentional, sudden glance does fall upon a Ghair Mahram woman then a man is forgiven for looking, with this condition that after the first glance, he immediately lowers his gaze. The reward for this is that Allāh ﷻ will grant him the sweetness of Imān.

Allāh ﷻ mentions اَبْصَارِهِمْ first and then فُرُوجَهُمْ, this is because the eyes are the introductory organ which entails the stepping stone for more evil. One should hence protect his gaze which will necessitate protection of the private parts too.

اَزْكَىٰ—One will be able to purify himself from all unlawful desires and control his temptations.

خَبِيْرٌ—Allāh ﷻ is All-Aware of the certain intentions e.g. good or bad that a person holds in the mind.

Modesty

وَقُل لِّلْمُؤْمِنَٰتِ يَغْضُضْنَ مِنْ أَبْصَٰرِهِنَّ وَيَحْفَظْنَ فُرُوجَهُنَّ وَلَا يُبْدِينَ زِينَتَهُنَّ إِلَّا مَا ظَهَرَ مِنْهَا وَلْيَضْرِبْنَ بِخُمُرِهِنَّ عَلَىٰ جُيُوبِهِنَّ وَلَا يُبْدِينَ زِينَتَهُنَّ إِلَّا لِبُعُولَتِهِنَّ أَوْ آبَآئِهِنَّ أَوْ آبَآءِ بُعُولَتِهِنَّ أَوْ أَبْنَآئِهِنَّ أَوْ أَبْنَآءِ بُعُولَتِهِنَّ أَوْ إِخْوَٰنِهِنَّ أَوْ بَنِىٓ إِخْوَٰنِهِنَّ أَوْ بَنِىٓ أَخَوَٰتِهِنَّ أَوْ نِسَآئِهِنَّ أَوْ مَا مَلَكَتْ أَيْمَٰنُهُنَّ أَوِ ٱلتَّٰبِعِينَ غَيْرِ أُو۟لِى ٱلْإِرْبَةِ مِنَ ٱلرِّجَالِ أَوِ ٱلطِّفْلِ ٱلَّذِينَ لَمْ يَظْهَرُوا۟ عَلَىٰ عَوْرَٰتِ ٱلنِّسَآءِ وَلَا يَضْرِبْنَ بِأَرْجُلِهِنَّ لِيُعْلَمَ مَا يُخْفِينَ مِن زِينَتِهِنَّ وَتُوبُوٓا۟ إِلَى ٱللَّهِ جَمِيعًا أَيُّهَ ٱلْمُؤْمِنُونَ لَعَلَّكُمْ تُفْلِحُونَ

"Say (O Muhammad) to the believing women that they must lower their gazes and guard their private parts and not expose their adornment except that which is apparent and to wrap their scarves over their chests and that they should not expose their adornment except to their husbands, their fathers, their husbands' fathers, their sons, their husbands' sons, their brothers, their brothers' sons, their sisters' sons, their women, that which their right hands possess, or those male attendants who have no physical desire, or children who are not yet aware of the private aspects of women. And let them not stamp their feet to make known what they conceal of their adornment. And turn to Allāh in repentance all of you, O believers, so that you (all) may achieve success." (24:31)

In this verse, Allāh is addressing and commanding the believing women through the Holy Prophet that they should not intentionally or in any unnecessary situation, look at any unknown men (Ghair Mahārim); rather they should instantly lower their gazes. If a woman protects her gaze, this will automatically necessitate protection of the private parts and refraining from other sins as well. As previously mentioned, the word مِنْ gives the meaning of تَبْعِيْض (partiality). This means that the believing women do not have to lower their gazes at all times e.g. whilst in the presence of Mahārim (this will be discussed further in detail).

وَلَا يُبْدِيْنَ زِيْنَتَهُنَّ—The Scholars of Tafsīr mention that the word زِيْنَةُ refers to the inner and outer beauty— the beauty of a woman's clothes and the beauty of the body.

A woman should not reveal any of the adorned parts of her body. This means she should not be leaving the house for example, wearing designer clothing which could possibly attract the attention of men. Secondly, a woman should not wear transparent, revealing clothing which would expose the shape of her body or such clothing that would reveal the adorned parts of a woman's body e.g. wearing a shirt in which the chest is visible or wearing a skirt in which the thighs are visible.

إِلَّا مَا ظَهَرَ مِنْهَا—Many Scholars of Tafsīr, such as Sayyidunā Abdullāh Ibn Abbās ؓ say this refers to اَلْوَجْهُ وَالْكَفَّيْنِ the face and the two palms. A woman has been granted permission to uncover certain adorned body parts e.g. the face, the hands up to the wrist and feet up to the ankles in normal situations. Wherever there is fear of Fitnah (temptation), then it is mandatory for a woman to cover these body parts as well.

Important Note: Some individuals are of the opinion that a woman does not need to cover the face, the hands up to the wrist and feet up to the ankles and use this particular verse as evidence. However, the correct opinion is that as Fitnah (temptation) is increasing and is at its greatest in this era, it is incumbent for a woman to cover the aforementioned body parts as well.

وَلْيَضْرِبْنَ بِخُمُرِهِنَّ عَلَىٰ جُيُوْبِهِنَّ —This particular upper part of the body (chest) is the most seductive and attractive. Therefore, Allāh ﷻ is heavily emphasising that the womenfolk should safeguard and cover this specific part of their body thoroughly in comparison to other parts. A woman may already be wearing her normal clothing; this is not sufficient. Rather over this, she should be wearing for example, another big shawl in order to cover this particular area of her body adequately.

The Kafn (shroud) normally consists of three pieces of cloth for a male. However, for a woman, the two extra pieces signify a great degree of importance in safeguarding her body parts and modesty - this is even when she has died. If a woman is alive and young, then one can imagine how much more crucial it is for her to cover herself appropriately.

Between a woman and her husband, a woman is permitted and should expose her adornment. Sayyidunā Abdullāh Ibn Abbās ؓ says, "Like the way I want my wife to beautify herself for me, she will also want me to beautify myself for her." The pitiful situation is that whilst in the presence of their husbands, women will present themselves in an unpleasant manner. At a wedding, when meeting friends or any other places, women will spend hours in front of the mirror beautifying themselves for those other than the husbands.

The father, brother, etc are all Mahārim for the woman. The general ruling is that in front of any Mahram, a woman should be fully covered from the neck to the knees. It is important that a woman still keeps utmost respect and modesty in front of any Mahārim or whilst in the presence of any women.

أَوۡ نِسَآئِهِنَّ -The Scholars of Tafsīr answer the question as to why Allāh ﷻ added the pronoun هِنَّ and did not just say نِسَآء. The Scholars mention that if there are Muslim women present, then the ruling is the same as Mahram men. However, if there are non Muslim women present then it is necessary to cover themselves just as it is necessary to cover in front of Ghair Mahārim.

أَوِ الطِّفۡلِ الَّذِيۡنَ لَمۡ يَظۡهَرُوۡا عَلٰى عَوۡرٰتِ النِّسَآءِ —Those immature children e.g. five or six year olds. If a woman needs to uncover her Hijāb etc in front of them, then she can do so. However, once they grow older and the woman knows that they are now mature enough to understand, then a woman should be careful not to uncover her certain body parts. Sayyidunā Abdullāh Ibn Umar ؓ used to be very careful to this extent that whenever there would be a small child, he would never engage in intimate relations with his wife in that same room. The reason for this is because it may be possible that the effects will come upon the child later on.

وَلَا يَضْرِبْنَ بِأَرْجُلِهِنَّ لِيُعْلَمَ مَا يُخْفِينَ مِنْ زِينَتِهِنَّ —This refers to any woman who may wear anklets, bangles or high heels in order to allure the attention of men; this intention of seduction is completely incorrect and is forbidden. A woman should not be uncovering any hidden adornment which could attract attention.

وَتُوبُوا إِلَى اللهِ جَمِيعًا أَيُّهَ الْمُؤْمِنُونَ لَعَلَّكُمْ تُفْلِحُونَ —Allāh ﷻ concludes the verse, after systematically mentioning all these important rulings, by saying all the believing men and women should seek repentance to Allāh ﷻ for all these mistakes which have been committed.

<u>Lesson:</u> These verses teach us that nobody is perfect or sinless, rather we are all to be blamed to some degree. We should all take heed from these above verses by sincerely asking forgiveness from Allāh ﷻ for all our sins and sincerely seeking Allāh's ﷻ assistance in helping us to implement bashfulness and Taqwa in our lives.

The Blame Game

وَتَفَقَّدَ الطَّيْرَ فَقَالَ مَا لِيَ لَا أَرَى الْهُدْهُدَ أَمْ كَانَ مِنَ الْغَآئِبِينَ

"And (once) he (Sulaimān) took attendance of the birds and said, 'How is it with me that I do not see the hoopoe - rather, is he among the absent?'" (27:20)

This verse is with regards to the story of Sayyidunā Sulaimān ﷺ. When Sayyidunā Sulaimān ﷺ realised that Hud-Hud (the hoopoe) was nowhere to be found, he said, مَا لِيَ لَا أَرَى الْهُدْهُدَ **"What is wrong with myself that I am unable to view Hud-Hud."**

The Scholars of Tafsīr mention that Sayyidunā Sulaimān ﷺ initially attributed the problem to himself—he thought to himself that it is my fault, my deficiency and negligence through which I am unable to see Hud-Hud.

This Qur'anic verse is teaching us a lesson that if we are carrying out any tasks and anything undesirable occurs, the first thing we should do is think to ourselves that there is something which we have done incorrectly due to which this mishap took place. In this day and age, we have a tendency of pointing the finger at others, whilst we want to always remain blame-free.

<u>Lesson:</u> We should contemplate over our own faults and never think we are guilt-free. Upon one occasion, Sayyidunā Umar ؓ was carry-

ing out his usual routine of patrolling the city of Madīnah Munawwarah in the evening. He saw a woman with her child who was continuously crying. Sayyidunā Umar ﷺ said, "What an evil mother you are by letting your child cry constantly!" She did not know she was talking to Sayyidunā Umar ﷺ and replied, "Amīrul Muminīn (leader of the believers) has stipulated an allowance for those children who are weaned off so I am trying to wean off my child." Upon hearing this, the Companions ﷺ mention Sayyidunā Umar ﷺ was weeping so excessively that they could not understand what he was reciting during the Fajr Salāh. After the Fajr Salāh, Sayyidunā Umar ﷺ stood upon the Mimbar (pulpit) saying, "Umar, the Amīrul Muminīn (Leader of the Believers) is not in front of you. Rather, Umar, the murderer is in front of you. I have killed so many children due to this law of mine." He attributed the "wrong doing" to himself and not to anyone else. Subhān-Allāh!

The Worldly Life

وَمَا هَٰذِهِ الْحَيَوٰةُ الدُّنْيَا إِلَّا لَهْوٌ وَلَعِبٌ وَإِنَّ الدَّارَ الْآخِرَةَ لَهِيَ الْحَيَوَانُ لَوْ كَانُوا يَعْلَمُونَ

"And this worldly life is nothing but an amusement/diversion and play. And indeed, the home of the Hereafter - that is the (eternal) life; only if they knew." (29:64)

The word لَهْوٌ refers to a benefit which is only useful for this life. For example, one may take up sport in order to stay healthy and fit. The word لَعِبٌ refers to a benefit which is neither useful in this life, neither in the Hereafter. For example, one may waste time playing video games, board games etc.

When we will face the Hereafter, we will say with regret,

$$يٰلَيْتَنِيْ قَدَّمْتُ لِحَيَاتِيْ$$

"'If only I put some good deeds forth for my life.'" (89:24)

Allāh ﷻ uses the word لِحَيَاتِيْ which implies that the Hereafter is the actual, eternal life. Anything we gain in this short lasting world will ultimately perish and will not come to any assistance in the Hereafter. Those who performed good actions in this world, Allāh ﷻ will say to them,

$$اِرْجِعِيْ إِلٰى رَبِّكِ رَاضِيَةً مَّرْضِيَّةً$$

"Return to your Lord, well-pleased and pleasing (to Him)" (89:28)

It is interesting to know the wording Allāh ﷻ has used in this verse. Allāh ﷻ used the verb اِرْجِعِيْ not اِذْهَبِيْ. Allāh ﷻ did not say 'go' but instead said 'return.' This demonstrates that our true house is situated in the Hereafter, not in this temporary world.

<u>Lesson</u>: We must not make this world a place where we are constantly in amusement and fulfilling our desires, but rather a place where

we reflect on our actions daily in order to improve our connection and relationship with Allāh ﷻ.

Conviction Upon a Verse

الٓمٓ غُلِبَتِ الرُّومُ فِىٓ أَدْنَى الْأَرْضِ وَهُم مِّنۢ بَعْدِ غَلَبِهِمْ سَيَغْلِبُونَ فِى بِضْعِ سِنِينَ لِلّٰهِ الْأَمْرُ مِن قَبْلُ وَمِنۢ بَعْدُ وَيَوْمَئِذٍ يَفْرَحُ الْمُؤْمِنُونَ بِنَصْرِ اللّٰهِ يَنصُرُ مَن يَشَآءُ وَهُوَ الْعَزِيزُ الرَّحِيمُ وَعْدَ اللّٰهِ لَا يُخْلِفُ اللّٰهُ وَعْدَهُ وَلٰكِنَّ أَكْثَرَ النَّاسِ لَا يَعْلَمُونَ

"Alif Lām Mīm. The Romans have been defeated. In the nearer land; and they after their defeat will triumph/overcome within a few years. To Allāh belongs the command before and after. And on that day the believers will rejoice with Allāh's help. He helps whomsoever He wills. And He is the Exalted in Might, the Merciful. It is a promise from Allāh. Allāh does not fail in His promise, but most of the people do not know." (30:1-6)

The two main superpowers at the time of the Holy Prophet ﷺ were the Romans and the Persians. The Romans held a similarity with the Muslims which was that both maintained belief in one God. Whenever the Persians would become victorious over the Romans, the polytheists of Makkah would take good fortune from that victory and would mock at the Muslims presuming that they would, in a similar manner, conquer the Muslims due to the polytheists of Makkah possessing a similarity with the Persians—which was that of worshipping idols.

During the fifth year of Prophethood, when the Holy Prophet ﷺ was forty-five years of age, the Persians heavily defeated the Romans and dominated many surrounding countries which were previously under the governance of Rome e.g. Syria, Palestine and Jordan. The triumph was to such an extent, that the leader of Rome, Caesar, was forced to take refuge in Constantinople. The polytheists of Makkah were enjoying the success of the Persians, simultaneously the verse was revealed,

$$\text{غُلِبَتِ الرُّومُ فِي أَدْنَى الْأَرْضِ}$$

"The Romans have been defeated in the nearer land." (30:2-3)

In the Qur'ān, Allāh ﷻ indicated towards an amazing prophecy through the verse,

$$\text{وَهُمْ مِّنْ بَعْدِ غَلَبِهِمْ سَيَغْلِبُونَ فِي بِضْعِ سِنِينَ}$$

"And they, after their defeat, will triumph/overcome within a few years." (30:3-4)

The Romans after their defeat, will regain their supremacy in a few years. Sayyidunā Abū Bakr ؓ relying on this particular verse, made a deal with a friend, that in five or six years, if the Romans defeat the Persians, you must give me a hundred camels. Conversely, if the Persians defeat the Romans, I will give you a hundred camels.

When this news reached the Holy Prophet ﷺ, he agreed with the deal Sayyidunā Abū Bakr ؓ made. However, the Holy Prophet ﷺ

said بِضْعٌ refers to three to nine years. The Holy Prophet ﷺ hence instructed Sayyidunā Abū Bakr ؓ to return to his friend in order to extend the deal to nine years; not five or six and to also increase the amount of camels to two hundred.

Just before the ninth year of this deal was about to finish, the Battle of Badr took place in which the Muslims won and at the same time, the battle between the Romans and Persians took place in which the Romans overcame the Persians.

يَفْرَحُ الْمُؤْمِنُوْنَ—The believers will rejoice refers to the double happiness the Muslims experienced.

اَلْعَزِيْزُ—Allāh ﷻ is All-Mighty as He turned a tremendous defeat into a victory.

اَلرَّحِيْمُ—Allāh ﷻ is All-Merciful as He helped the Muslims out of His infinite kindness.

When Sayyidunā Abū Bakr ؓ received the camels, the Holy Prophet ﷺ told Sayyidunā Abū Bakr ؓ to give them camels to the poor people. The reason for this was due to the status he held - even though gambling was permissible at that time, but because it was soon going to end, Allāh ﷻ did not want Sayyidunā Abū Bakr ؓ to take anything that would become forbidden afterwards.

Lesson: This incident clearly shows us the reliance we need to inculcate upon Allāh ﷻ and His plans for us. Sayyidunā Abdullāh Ibn Mas'ūd ؓ was on his death bed and Sayyidunā Uthmān ؓ asked him, "You have not left any wealth for your daughters; what will they do?" Sayyidunā Abdullāh Ibn Mas'ūd ؓ replied, "They recite Sūrah Wāqi'ah every night - that should be sufficient." This is because the Holy Prophet ﷺ said,

$$\text{مَنْ قَرَأَ سُورَةَ الْوَاقِعَةِ فِي كُلِّ لَيْلَةٍ لَمْ تُصِبْهُ فَاقَةٌ أَبَدًا}$$

"The person who recites Sūrah Wāqi'ah every night, poverty will not afflict him." (Baihaqi in Shu'abul Īmān)

I have instructed my daughters to recite it every night.
May Allāh ﷻ grant us all such conviction regarding Him. Āmīn.

Sad State of Affairs

$$\text{يَعْلَمُونَ ظَاهِرًا مِّنَ الْحَيَاةِ الدُّنْيَا وَهُمْ عَنِ الْآخِرَةِ هُمْ غَافِلُونَ}$$

"They know the apparent things of the worldly life, but they are negligent of the Hereafter." (30:7)

Allāh ﷻ is referring to the rejectors of Islām in this verse. Unfortunately, this verse can be applicable to us Muslims in this day and age. If we ask the youngsters today to mention all eleven players in a football team they will instantly mention them all. On the other hand, if we ask them to mention the ten Companions who were granted the glad tidings of Jannah or the children of the Holy Prophet ﷺ, they will hesitate and become completely speechless. Nowadays, we have no time for Salāh or time to learn the Qur'ān.

Lesson: We need to familiarise ourselves with the Sīrah (biography) of the Holy Prophet ﷺ, the Sahābah ؓ and our pious predecessors. We have filled our minds with all the artificial things of the worldly life and forgotten the Dīn (religion). To a certain extent; it is fine to know certain benefits of the world, but we need to give ultimate priority to our Dīn (religion).

Signs of Allāh ﷻ

وَمِنْ اٰيٰتِهٖ أَنْ خَلَقَكُمْ مِّنْ تُرَابٍ ثُمَّ إِذَا أَنْتُمْ بَشَرٌ تَنْتَشِرُوْنَ

"And from Allāh's signs is that He created you from soil then you were created as human beings." (30:20)

There are two types of signs:

تَكْوِيْنِيَّة - The creation e.g. the heavens and the earth etc.

تَنْزِيْلِيَّة - The Qur'ān

Sayyidunā Ādam ؑ was created from soil and from Sayyidunā Ādam ؑ (one human) came Sayyidah Hawwā ؑ which led to the creation of all mankind.

$$\text{وَمِنْ اٰيٰتِهٖٓ أَنْ خَلَقَ لَكُمْ مِّنْ أَنْفُسِكُمْ أَزْوَاجًا لِّتَسْكُنُوْٓا إِلَيْهَا وَجَعَلَ بَيْنَكُمْ مَّوَدَّةً وَّرَحْمَةً ۚ إِنَّ فِيْ ذٰلِكَ لَاٰيٰتٍ لِّقَوْمٍ يَّتَفَكَّرُوْنَ}$$

"And from Allāh's signs is that He created for you, from yourselves, wives so that you may live in tranquility and peace with them and He placed between you both affection and mercy. Indeed therein are many signs for those people who reflect." (30:21)

Occasionally, the word مِنْ gives the meaning of تَبْعِيْض (partiality). In the coming six verses, Allāh ﷻ is elaborating upon His many signs bestowed upon the creation.

From the left rib of Sayyidunā Ādam علیہ السلام, Sayyidah Hawwā علیہا السلام was created. This means that a man should keep his wife close to his heart. Allāh ﷻ did not create Sayyidah Hawwā علیہا السلام from the foot of Sayyidunā Ādam علیہ السلام so that women would be trampled over and abused by their husbands! The verse is instructing us to honour and respect our wives.

لِتَسْكُنُوْٓا إِلَيْهَا - The Qur'ān is clearly stating that when we see our wives, all the tension should leave. The sad reality is that in this day and age, as love is non-existent, tension soon builds up. Tranquility in a marriage should become our main motive and objective.

Allāh ﷻ has mentioned مَوَدَّةً (love) which indicates towards the beginning stages of the marriage and رَحْمَةً (mercy) indicates towards the latter stages of the marriage. In the beginning stages of marriage, mainly physical act of love is transferred between couples and in the latter stages, usually more mercy and affection is apparent in an elderly couple.

وَمِنْ ءَايَٰتِهِۦ خَلْقُ ٱلسَّمَٰوَٰتِ وَٱلْأَرْضِ وَٱخْتِلَٰفُ أَلْسِنَتِكُمْ وَأَلْوَٰنِكُمْ إِنَّ فِى ذَٰلِكَ لَءَايَٰتٍ لِّلْعَٰلِمِينَ

"And from Allāh's signs is the creation of the heavens and the earth and the diversity of your languages and colours. Indeed therein are signs for all mankind." (30:22)

أَلْسِنَتِكُمْ وَأَلْوَٰنِكُمْ - From amongst Allāh's ﷻ signs, He created innumerable different complexions, languages and within all them languages lie so many different dialects. The parents could be speaking one particular language, but the children may speak completely different dialects and languages.

If we join this verse with another,

قُلْ أَبِٱللَّهِ وَءَايَٰتِهِۦ وَرَسُولِهِۦ كُنتُمْ تَسْتَهْزِءُونَ

"Say (O Muhammad), is it Allāh and His verses and His Messenger that you were mocking?" (9:65)

We come to learn that mocking at anyone's language or anyone's skin colour is totally forbidden and could possibly lead a person towards Kufr (disbelief) because we are ultimately mocking at a sign of Allāh ﷻ.

$$\text{وَمِنْ آيَاتِهِ مَنَامُكُم بِاللَّيْلِ وَالنَّهَارِ وَابْتِغَاؤُكُم مِّن فَضْلِهِ إِنَّ فِي ذَٰلِكَ لَآيَاتٍ لِّقَوْمٍ يَسْمَعُونَ}$$

"And from Allāh's signs is your sleep during the night and day and your seeking of His bounty. Indeed therein are signs for people who listen." (30:23)

مَنَامُكُم بِاللَّيْلِ وَالنَّهَارِ - An amazing blessing Allāh ﷻ has gifted to His creation is the ability to see dreams whilst sleeping. For example, an individual could be sleeping in England whilst dreaming they are performing Tawāf in Makkah Mukarramah. A person is alive whilst sleeping whilst dead at the same time.

وَابْتِغَاؤُكُم مِّن فَضْلِهِ - When an individual is sleeping, they have no idea what is going on around them; they are not even aware of their own movements. However, when they wake up, they become frantic in search of their sustenance. We will see the people lined up waiting for the buses to go to work with the same objective in mind; seeking His sustenance.

$$\text{وَمِنْ آيَاتِهِ يُرِيكُمُ الْبَرْقَ خَوْفًا وَطَمَعًا وَيُنَزِّلُ مِنَ السَّمَاءِ مَاءً فَيُحْيِي بِهِ الْأَرْضَ بَعْدَ مَوْتِهَا إِنَّ فِي ذَٰلِكَ لَآيَاتٍ لِّقَوْمٍ يَعْقِلُونَ}$$

> "And from Allāh's signs is that He shows you lightening (causing) fear and aspiration and He sends down rain from the sky by which He brings to life the earth after its lifelessness. Indeed therein are signs for those who possess intellect." (30:24)

Lightening creates fear within people as it could be the cause of many deaths. On the other hand, lightening gives people hope because usually after lightening comes rain which results in the growth of many plants and vegetation.

It is an immense favour of Allāh ﷻ that He sends down rain by which flowers and trees blossom and the earth becomes fertile in the spring and summer after becoming barren during the winter and autumn seasons.

يَعْقِلُوْنَ — Those who possess intellect will understand the cycle of vegetation in the different seasons e.g. autumn, winter, spring etc.

وَمِنْ اٰيٰتِهٖۤ اَنْ تَقُوْمَ السَّمَآءُ وَالْاَرْضُ بِاَمْرِهٖ ثُمَّ اِذَا دَعَاكُمْ دَعْوَةً مِّنَ الْاَرْضِ اِذَاۤ اَنْتُمْ تَخْرُجُوْنَ

> "And from Allāh's signs is that the heaven and earth remain by His command. Then when He will call you with a (single) call from the earth, you will immediately come forth." (30:25)

It is a bounty of Allāh ﷻ that He has provided the creation with such a vast land which we are able to live upon and the sky for us to view; for so many years and generations, there has been no need to repair a single crack of any sort! Everything remains faultless and flawless.

All is in existence according to Allāh's ﷻ command. When the command from Allāh ﷻ will come to put an end to the earth, all those beautiful things within the world will collapse and be destroyed.

إِذَا دَعَاكُمْ دَعْوَةً – This 'call' is referring to the Day of Judgement. We will all come out from the earth in order to be summoned together in the court of Allāh ﷻ.

Lesson: After pondering over all these signs, an individual will reach the conclusion that Allāh ﷻ is One. In another verse, Allāh ﷻ mentions,

$$\text{إِنْ تَعُدُّوا نِعْمَتَ اللّٰهِ لَا تُحْصُوهَا}$$

"If you (try to) count the bounties of Allāh, you cannot enumerate them all." (14:34)

Allāh ﷻ has favoured us with so many blessings yet we still complain and are very ungrateful. Let us all say Alhamdulillāh and praise Allāh ﷻ for everything we have been given. In Sūrah Ibrāhīm, Allāh ﷻ mentions,

$$\text{لَئِنْ شَكَرْتُمْ لَأَزِيدَنَّكُمْ وَلَئِنْ كَفَرْتُمْ إِنَّ عَذَابِي لَشَدِيدٌ}$$

"If you express gratitude, I shall certainly give you more and if you are ungrateful, then My punishment is severe." (14:7)

Wisdom of Luqmān

وَلَقَدْ اٰتَيْنَا لُقْمٰنَ الْحِكْمَةَ أَنِ اشْكُرْ لِلّٰهِ وَمَنْ يَشْكُرْ فَإِنَّمَا يَشْكُرُ لِنَفْسِهٖ وَمَنْ كَفَرَ فَإِنَّ اللّٰهَ غَنِيٌّ حَمِيْدٌ

"And We certainly gave wisdom to Luqmān and said, "Be grateful to Allāh" and whoever is grateful is in fact grateful for his own benefit and whoever is ungrateful, then indeed Allāh is free of all needs, worthy of all praise." (31:12)

Sayyidunā Luqmān is amongst those great men whom Allāh ﷻ had blessed. He is also known as Luqmān Hakīm because of the many wisdoms he possessed. Wahab Ibn Munabbah ؓ (a famous Tābi'ī) states, "I have read more than 10,000 words of wisdom of Luqmān."

There is a difference of opinion as to whether Sayyidunā Luqmān was a Prophet or not. The preferred opinion is that he was a great Walī (saint) of Allāh ﷻ but not a Prophet. It is said that he was living during the era of Sayyidunā Dāwūd ؑ.

Sayyidunā Luqmān himself mentions, "I have met 4,000 Prophets and sat in their company." Someone once asked him regarding the main wisdom he learnt from these Prophets? He summarised it in eight points:

1. Protect the heart during Salāh i.e. pray with full submission and concentration.

2. Protect the tongue when seated in a gathering.

3. Protect the throat whilst sitting on the tablecloth i.e. ensure nothing unlawful is eaten.

4. Protect the eyes when visiting someone's house i.e. the gaze should be lowered and should not fall upon any Ghair Mahram (those whom one is permitted to marry).

<u>The fifth and sixth are to always forget</u>

5. Forget that you have done any good to someone, therefore the sincerity of the deed remains.

6. If someone behaves in an unkind manner towards you, forget they have done bad to you—forgive and forget.

<u>The seventh and eighth are to never forget</u>

7. The Dhikr of Allāh ﷻ.

8. Death.

Sayyidunā Luqmān's master once instructed him to slaughter a goat and present the best part of the goat, so Sayyidunā Luqmān presented the heart and the tongue. After a few days, his master instructed him again to present the worst part of the goat, so Sayyidunā

Luqmān presented the tongue and heart. The master said, "This is very strange, you brought the same parts twice!" Sayyidunā Luqmān replied, "If the heart and tongue are used in the correct manner, then they are the best parts. However, if the heart and tongue are used in the incorrect manner, then they will become the worst parts."

Upon another occasion, Sayyidunā Luqmān's master ordered him to bring a fruit from the garden. Sayyidunā Luqmān thus handed his master a fruit which consequently tasted bitter. His master then asked him to bring a sweet fruit. Sayyidunā Luqmān handed another fruit but it again tasted bitter. This happened for the third time which made his master become very angry with him. The master said, "Do you not know which tree is sweet and which tree is bitter!?" Sayyidunā Luqmān replied, "You gave me the responsibility to look after the garden, not to eat from the garden otherwise I would have eaten one and presented it to you." His master asked, "Until today have you not eaten a single fruit from this garden?" Sayyidunā Luqmān replied, "Never."

Whilst advising his son, Sayyidunā Luqmān told him, "I have travelled and taken the burden of metal, iron and those things which are very heavy on my back. However, there is no burden more heavier than taking someone else's Ihsān (favour) upon yourself; do not take favours from anyone else.

Similarly, it was once asked to Sayyidunā Luqmān after he was advising a huge gathering of people, "Were you not a shepherd before?" Sayyidunā Luqmān replied, "Indeed I was." The person then asked, "How did you attain such a high status?" He replied because of two reasons:

1. Protecting the tongue i.e. always speaking the truth.

2. Not involving myself in other peoples' matters i.e. not to be involved/engrossed in useless talk.

<u>Lesson</u>: We should ponder over the wisdom of Sayyidunā Luqmān and try to implement them in our lives. One recurring theme is that of protecting the tongue, therefore, we should always speak the truth no matter what the circumstance may be.

Knowledge of the Unseen

إِنَّ اللَّهَ عِنْدَهُ عِلْمُ السَّاعَةِ وَيُنَزِّلُ الْغَيْثَ وَيَعْلَمُ مَا فِي الْأَرْحَامِ وَمَا تَدْرِيْ نَفْسٌ مَّاذَا تَكْسِبُ غَدًا وَمَا تَدْرِيْ نَفْسٌ بِأَيِّ أَرْضٍ تَمُوْتُ إِنَّ اللَّهَ عَلِيْمٌ خَبِيْرٌ

"Indeed, Allāh (alone) has knowledge of the Hour and He sends down the rain and He knows what is in the wombs. No soul knows what he will earn tomorrow and no soul knows in which land he will die. Indeed Allāh is All Knowing, All Aware." (31:34)

This verse was revealed when the Holy Prophet ﷺ was asked regarding these five questions:

1. When is the Day of Judgement? In the Holy Qur'ān, Allāh ﷻ mentions,

$$\text{إِنَّ السَّاعَةَ آتِيَةٌ أَكَادُ أُخْفِيهَا لِتُجْزَىٰ كُلُّ نَفْسٍ بِمَا تَسْعَىٰ}$$

"Indeed, the Hour (the Day of Judgement) is coming. I shall conceal it, so that every soul may be recompensed according to that for which it strives." (20:15)

Allāh ﷻ mentions that He would have hidden the knowledge regarding the Day of Judgement from Himself if He could; although nothing is hidden from Allāh ﷻ. This explains the extreme level of knowledge of which only Allāh ﷻ knows. Within the famous Hadīth, Hadīth Jibrīl, Jibrīl ؑ questioned the Holy Prophet ﷺ concerning the Day of Judgement. The Holy Prophet ﷺ replied,

$$\text{مَا الْمَسْئُوْلُ عَنْهَا بِأَعْلَمَ مِنَ السَّائِلِ}$$

"The person who is being asked has no better knowledge than the person who is asking." (Bukhārī)

Only Allāh ﷻ has knowledge of the Day of Judgement.

2. When will it rain?

Upon the subject of Allāh ﷻ sending down rain, the question could be raised that in this day and age, those who predict the weather forecast, do they have knowledge of the unseen? i.e. if it will rain tomorrow? The answer is that it is a weather forecast, not knowledge of the weather; it is a mere prediction. When it is said Allāh ﷻ sends down the rain, it refers to every minute drop of rain which will fall. Only Allāh ﷻ alone holds knowledge of this.

3.   What is in the mother's womb?

With regards to knowing what is in the womb, the objection could be raised that doctors and nurses have the knowledge or the gender of the child, therefore apparently, it seems as if this is going against the Qur'ān. The answer is that doctors and nurses have the knowledge through the latest technology which can sometimes be incorrect.

In this verse, the letter ما has been used - this means every minute detail regarding the child: will the child live or die, will the child be intelligent, will the child be of dark or light complexion, will they be obedient, disobedient etc. Only Allāh ﷻ holds knowledge of all these things.

4.   What will a person earn/do tomorrow?

A person should not constantly think about the future as they do not know if they will be alive. Yesterday is history, tomorrow is a mystery and today is present - a gift. Let us utilise the current day instead of waiting for the next day and making false promises of saying, "Tomorrow I will do this." A person may be working, thinking they have a permanent job however, the next day that same person may be sacked and as a result, jobless.

5. Which land will a person die?

It is not allowed to purchase a particular plot of land for ones grave. The Fuqahā (jurists) state it is Makrūh (disliked) to dig or purchase one's own grave because a person does not know if they will die at that particular place. A person is allowed to buy the Kafan (shroud) and fragrance before his death.

There is the famous incident which Imām Mālik ﷺ encountered regarding this specific verse.

One night, he saw the Holy Prophet ﷺ in his dream and mentioned to the Holy Prophet ﷺ regarding his intention to visit Makkah Mukarramah in order to perform Umrah. He asked the Holy Prophet ﷺ concerning how many days left (i.e. until he passes away). The Holy Prophet ﷺ showed his blessed five fingers. When Imām Mālik ﷺ awoke that morning, he became very distressed as he did not know what the dream (five fingers) meant—whether it was five days, five weeks, five months, five years etc. He narrated his dream to the student of Imām Muhammad Ibn Sīrīn ﷺ—a great scholar and expert regarding the science of interpreting dreams. The interpretation of the dream was this verse i.e. the five fingers refers to the above five mentioned things, which even the Holy Prophet ﷺ has no knowledge of.

Imām Mālik ؓ held extreme love and respect for the blessed city of Madīnah Munawwarah, that after the completion of his Hajj, he never wanted to leave the blessed city as he heavily desired for his death to take place within Madīnah Munawwarah. Before reciting any Ahādīth, he would have a Ghusl (bath) and apply fragrance. If he was walking, he never used to narrate any Ahādīth, but rather if someone asked him, he would sit down and narrate the Hadīth in his Majlis (gathering). His respect was to such a great degree that whenever the need arose to relieve himself, he would do so outside the boundaries of Madīnah Munawwarah whilst at the same time, keeping his feet inside the boundaries. Due to this immense respect, it is said that he would see the Holy Prophet ﷺ every night in his dream.

Lesson: A person should not dwell into those matters which he has no knowledge of. Instead, one should leave this knowledge to Allāh ﷻ. Our objective in this world is to worship Allāh ﷻ therefore we should worry about our death and perform as many good actions as we can in this world. We should not constantly think about the next day but rather we should work for the current day.

The Seal of all Prophets

مَا كَانَ مُحَمَّدٌ أَبَا أَحَدٍ مِّن رِّجَالِكُمْ وَلَٰكِن رَّسُولَ اللَّهِ وَخَاتَمَ النَّبِيِّنَ وَكَانَ اللَّهُ بِكُلِّ شَيْءٍ عَلِيمًا

"Muhammad is not the father of any one of your men, but he is a Messenger of Allāh and the last of the Prophets. And Allāh is Knowing of all things." (33:40)

Those within the era of the Holy Prophet ﷺ used to call the servant of the Holy Prophet ﷺ, Zaid Ibn Muhammad ؓ instead of his actual name; Zaid Ibn Hārithah ؓ. The verse was revealed to clearly emphasise and explain that the Holy Prophet ﷺ has no mature sons and also that the Holy Prophet ﷺ will have no mature sons after him i.e. sons who will live after him.

The question could be raised as to why the word Rijāl (plural form for men) was used. The answer is because the word Rijāl refers to those individuals who have reached the age of puberty. This clearly indicates that all of the Holy Prophet's ﷺ male children passed away in childhood, not adulthood. None of the sons of the Holy Prophet ﷺ reached the age of puberty.

There are three different viewpoints regarding how many sons the Holy Prophet ﷺ had:

Those who opine the Holy Prophet ﷺ had four sons mention, Qāsim, Tayyib, Tāhir and Ibrāhīm ؇.

Those who opine the Holy Prophet ﷺ had three sons mention, Qāsim, Tayyib and Ibrāhīm ؇.

Those who opine the Holy Prophet ﷺ had two sons mention: Qāsim and Ibrāhīm ؇ (Tayyib and Tāhir were other titles given to Qāsim ؇)

The majority of scholars agree, including Mufti Shafī Sāhib ؇ that the correct opinion is that the Holy Prophet ﷺ had only two sons - Qāsim and Ibrāhīm ؇.

<u>Lesson:</u> From this verse, we are given clear evidence that the Holy Prophet ﷺ is the Last Prophet. Thus any allegations that are present i.e. those who claim Prophethood after him are completely wrong and false. We should take it as a huge blessing to be within the nation of the Last Prophet and we should remember Allāh ﷻ is All-Knowing of every thing i.e. the huge wisdom behind the Holy Prophet ﷺ not having any male children.

Manners

يَا أَيُّهَا الَّذِينَ آمَنُوا لَا تَدْخُلُوا بُيُوتَ النَّبِيِّ إِلَّا أَن يُؤْذَنَ لَكُمْ إِلَىٰ طَعَامٍ غَيْرَ نَاظِرِينَ إِنَاهُ وَلَٰكِنْ إِذَا دُعِيتُمْ فَادْخُلُوا فَإِذَا طَعِمْتُمْ فَانتَشِرُوا وَلَا مُسْتَأْنِسِينَ لِحَدِيثٍ إِنَّ ذَٰلِكُمْ كَانَ يُؤْذِي النَّبِيَّ فَيَسْتَحْيِي مِنكُمْ وَاللَّهُ لَا يَسْتَحْيِي مِنَ الْحَقِّ

"O you who believe, do not enter the houses of the Prophet, except only when you are invited for a meal, without awaiting for its preparation. But when you are invited, then enter. Then once you have had the meal, disperse without seeking to remain for conversation. This conduct of yours troubles the Prophet, but he feels shy of dismissing you, but Allāh is not shy of the truth." (33:53)

This verse was revealed regarding a specific incident: the Holy Prophet's ﷺ marriage to Sayyidah Zainab Bint Jahsh ؓ. When the marriage took place, the Holy Prophet ﷺ invited the Sahābah ؓ to partake of some food. A few of the Sahābah ؓ did not realise that the Holy Prophet ﷺ was newly wed and wanted to spend time with his new wife. Thus majority of the Sahābah ؓ had left, but a few remained behind and lingered. In that era, the houses consisted of virtually one room therefore, there was very little space. Sayyidah Zainab Bint Jahsh ؓ had to sit in one corner facing the wall throughout the Walimah. It should be noted that this was an unintentional action of the Companions ؓ.

Out of modesty, the Holy Prophet ﷺ repeatedly walked in and out of his house and was troubled as he could not tell his respected Saḥābah ؓ to leave. This verse was simultaneously revealed which mentioned the inconvenience which was given to the Holy Prophet ﷺ. Although the Holy Prophet ﷺ out of respect and modesty did not say anything, Allāh ﷻ openly revealed this verse.

This verse is not only with regards to the etiquettes of entering the Holy Prophet's ﷺ house, but it includes the etiquettes of entering anyone's house.

Firstly, the verse mentions أَنْ يُؤْذَنَ لَكُمْ—entering the house when you have been given permission to enter. One should knock on the door three times and politely ask, "Can I enter?" If after three times the person does not answer, one should leave and not continue knocking; even if it seems that the person is in the house.

The value of time is also hinted in this verse through the words, غَيْرَ نَاظِرِينَ (without awaiting). The Holy Qur'ān mentions do not wait for the food to be cooked, rather come when the food is ready. For example in weddings, usually the time the food will be served is mentioned hence, come when the food will be ready and do not waste time chatting and gossiping. By continuously waiting, the time for Salāh usually expires and precious time, which could have been spent in the Dhikr of Allāh ﷻ, is wasted. Do not come at twelve o'clock and wait hours for one plate of rice!

Lesson: In terms of revelation, it was with regards to the Holy Prophet ﷺ, but the command is general for everyone. Let us keep in mind and adopt these manners & etiquettes when entering into a person's house. The Qur'ān mentions,

$$\text{وَإِنْ قِيلَ لَكُمُ ارْجِعُوْا فَارْجِعُوْا هُوَ أَزْكَىٰ لَكُمْ}$$

"And if it is said to you, 'Go back', then go back. This is more purifying for you." (24:28)

If someone does not open the door, we should not get offended as it is in fact more purifying - meaning it will take away the ego from within us and take a huge spiritual illness; pride out of our hearts.

Status of the Holy Prophet ﷺ

$$\text{إِنَّ اللّٰهَ وَمَلٰئِكَتَهُ يُصَلُّوْنَ عَلَى النَّبِيِّ يَا أَيُّهَا الَّذِيْنَ اٰمَنُوْا صَلُّوْا عَلَيْهِ وَسَلِّمُوْا تَسْلِيْمًا}$$

"Indeed, Allāh and His Angels confer blessings to the Prophet. O you who believe, confer blessings upon him and send your Salām (greeting) to him in abundance." (33:56)

Allāh ﷻ mentions His blessed name first, then the Angels, then the believers to signify the importance of sending salutations upon the Holy Prophet ﷺ. In the Holy Qur'ān, Allāh ﷻ commands the Angels to prostrate to Sayyidunā Ādam عليه السلام in order to raise his status. However in this verse, Allāh ﷻ Himself raises the status of the Holy Prophet ﷺ which indicates towards his lofty status. Also, the fact that Allāh ﷻ Himself constantly sends salutations, we are instructed to do the same i.e. send salutations upon the Holy Prophet ﷺ - this particular salutation is specific to only the Holy Prophet ﷺ and not to any other Prophet.

If we view the verse from a grammatical point of view, we come to realise three things:

1. Firstly, the word اِنَّ has been used to display emphasis.
2. Secondly, مَلٰٓئِكَتَهٗ refers to all the Angels in general.

3. Thirdly, the word يُصَلُّوْنَ has come in the present and future tense which gives the meaning of continuity—sending salutations constantly/in abundance all the time.

The Four Meanings of the Verb صَلَّىٰ

1. When the verb صَلَّىٰ comes with the word Allāh ﷻ, the meaning is of Rahmah (mercy).

2. When the verb صَلَّىٰ comes with the word مَلَائِكَة (angles), the meaning is of Istighfār (repentance).

3. When the verb صَلَّىٰ comes with اَلَّذِيْنَ اٰمَنُوْا (the believers), the meaning is of sending Durūd (salutations).

4. When the verb صَلَّىٰ comes with anything else for example trees, plants etc. the meaning is of Tasbīh (glorification).

The different stages of sending salutations upon the Holy Prophet ﷺ

صَلُّوْا is an imperative verb, therefore the Mufassirūn (Scholars of Tafsīr) & Muhaddithūn (Scholars of Hadīth) derive the ruling that it is Fardh (obligatory) to send Durūd upon the Holy Prophet ﷺ at least once in an individual's lifetime. If a person does not act upon this imperative, he will become sinful.

It is Wājib (necessary) to send salutations upon the Holy Prophet ﷺ at least once whilst sitting in a gathering whereby the Holy Prophet's ﷺ name has been mentioned frequently.

According to Imām Abu Hanīfah ﷺ, it is Sunnah Muakkadah (an emphasised Sunnah) to send salutations upon the Holy Prophet ﷺ whilst performing Salāh i.e. after reciting the Tashahhud. Other Scholars opine it obligatory or necessary to send salutations upon the Holy Prophet ﷺ in this instance.

It is Mustahab (preferable) to send salutations upon the Holy Prophet ﷺ in abundance and whenever the Holy Prophet's ﷺ name has been mentioned.

It is Makrūh (disliked) to send salutations upon the Holy Prophet ﷺ before starting one's business to impress one's nobility amongst the masses with the wrong intention.

Virtues of Durūd

Durūd is that particular distinct action which makes both the Kirāman Kātibīn busy simultaneously - the Angel stipulated upon the right shoulder is engrossed in writing the good deeds whilst the angel stipulated upon the left shoulder is busy erasing the sins. By sending just one Durūd upon the Holy Prophet ﷺ, the Angel upon the right shoulder will write ten good deeds for an individual and the angel upon the left shoulder will erase ten sins which an individual may have committed. Unfortunately, we regard sending Durūd as a minor action, thus we give no importance to sending salutations upon the Holy Prophet ﷺ.

Furthermore, ten Rahmah (mercy) will descend upon a person and he will obtain ten further ranks in Paradise. The Ahādīth makes mention that the person closest to the Holy Prophet ﷺ will be the one who sent salutations in abundance. The stingy person is he who does not send salutations when the Holy Prophet's ﷺ name is mentioned,

$$\text{اِنَّ اَوْلَى النَّاسِ بِيْ يَوْمَ الْقِيَامَةِ اَكْثَرُهُمْ عَلَيَّ صَلَاةً}$$

"The person closest to me on the Day of Judgement is the one who sends the most salutations upon me." (Tirmizi)

$$\text{اَلْبَخِيْلُ الَّذِيْ مَنْ ذُكِرْتُ عِنْدَهُ فَلَمْ يُصَلِّ عَلَيَّ}$$

"The stingy person is the one before whom I am mentioned, and he does not send salutations upon me." (Tirmizi)

Sayyidunā Ka'b Ibn Ujra ؓ narrates that the Holy Prophet ﷺ was once asked regarding how much time should be spent performing Durūd in the daily Ma'mūlāt (practises)? The Holy Prophet ﷺ replied, "How ever much is desired". The Companion ؓ firstly mentioned, "I will dedicate one quarter of my daily Ma'mūlāt for Durūd." The Holy Prophet ﷺ replied, "Māshā-Allāh! very good. If you recite more, it will be even better." The Companion ؓ then mentioned, "I will dedicate one third of my daily Ma'mūlāt for Durūd." The Holy Prophet ﷺ replied, "Māshā-Allāh! very good. If you recite more, it will be even better." The Companion ؓ subsequently mentioned, "I will dedicate one half of my daily Ma'mūlāt for Durūd." The Holy Prophet ﷺ replied, "Māshā-Allāh! very good. If you recite more, it will be even better."

The Companion ؓ then mentioned, "I will dedicate two thirds of my daily Ma'mūlāt for Durūd." The Holy Prophet ﷺ replied, "Māshā-Allāh! very good. If you recite more, it will be even better." The Companion ؓ lastly mentioned, "I will dedicate all of my daily Ma'mūlāt for Durūd; I will not recite any other Dhikr." The Holy Prophet ﷺ replied, "Allāh ﷻ will fulfill all your needs and will remove all your worries." This Hadīth thus clearly explains the reward and benefits of sending Durūd.

Once someone saw Imām Shāfi'ī ؒ in a dream and asked how he faced Allāh ﷻ (i.e. after his death). Imām Shāfi'ī ؒ replied, there was one specific Durūd which I used to pray, because of which Allāh ﷻ forgave me. The person asked, "What is it (the Durūd)?" Imām Shāfi'ī ؒ replied,

$$\text{اَللّٰهُمَّ صَلِّ عَلٰى مُحَمَّدٍ كُلَّمَا ذَكَرَهُ الذَّاكِرُوْنَ اَللّٰهُمَّ صَلِّ عَلٰى مُحَمَّدٍ كُلَّمَا غَفَلَ عَنْ ذِكْرِهِ الْغَافِلُوْنَ}$$

If a person has zeal for reciting Durūd, they should refer to Fadhāil Durūd—written by Shaykhul Hadīth, Shaykh Muhammad Zakariyyā ؒ.

Lesson: It is mentioned in a Hadīth,

اَلْمَرْءُ مَعَ مَنْ أَحَبَّ

"A person will be with the one whom he loves (on the Day of Judgement)." (Muslim)

If we claim to love the Holy Prophet ﷺ, we should continuously send Durūd upon him so that we may be resurrected with him on the Day of Judgement and receive his blessed intercession.

Nikāh and Taqwa

يَا أَيُّهَا الَّذِيْنَ اٰمَنُوا اتَّقُوا اللهَ وَقُوْلُوْا قَوْلًا سَدِيْدًا يُّصْلِحْ لَكُمْ أَعْمَالَكُمْ وَيَغْفِرْ لَكُمْ ذُنُوْبَكُمْ وَمَنْ يُّطِعِ اللهَ وَرَسُوْلَهُ فَقَدْ فَازَ فَوْزًا عَظِيْمًا

"O you who believe, fear Allāh and speak words of appropriate justice. (If you do so) Allāh will correct your deeds for your benefit and forgive your sins for you. Whoever obeys Allāh and His Messenger has certainly achieved a great success." (33:70-71)

These famous verses are read within the Khutbah (sermon) of a Nikāh (marriage). These verses have a common theme which is of Taqwa (God consciousness).

Someone once asked Sayyidunā Hasan Ibn Ali ﷺ that his daughter was of a marriageable age, hence who should he get his daughter married to? He replied,

زَوِّجْهَا مَنْ يَّخَافُ اللهَ ، فَإِنْ أَحَبَّهَا أَكْرَمَهَا ، وَإِنْ أَبْغَضَهَا لَمْ يَظْلِمْهَا

"Get her married to a person who fears Allāh ﷺ. If he loves her, he will respect her and if he dislikes her, he will not oppress her; he will not beat or swear at her etc. due to possessing the fear of Allāh ﷺ."

وَقُوْلُوْا قَوْلًا سَدِيْدًا - O you who believe, now you are about to say yes i.e. قَبِلْتُهَا (I have accepted) or نَكَحْتُهَا (I have married); think deeply! Accept the woman you intend to marry in the correct manner - do not marry with the intention of making a mockery or with the intention of causing any trouble or mischief. If you have said it properly, He (Allāh ﷺ) will amend your deeds and forgive your sins.

Firstly, Allāh ﷺ is commanding us to adopt Taqwa when taking His blessed name. It is through taking His name, that the two individuals become permissible for one another.

Secondly, Allāh ﷺ is commanding us to fear our relatives. The reason is because we should not let it be that we have a new mother/father in law thus we forget our own mother/father. We should not let it be that we have new sister and brother in laws hence we forget our own brothers and sisters. We should always bear in mind,

$$\text{إِنَّ اللّٰهَ كَانَ عَلَيْكُمْ رَقِيبًا}$$

"Allāh is ever watchful over you." (4:1)

<u>Lesson</u>: When searching for a suitable partner, a person should always give preference to a partner who is more practicing with regards to the Dīn (religion) of Allāh ﷻ. We should not be prioritising wealth, beauty or lineage as all this will eventually come to an end; beauty is skin deep! In one Hadīth it mentions,

$$\text{اَلدُّنْيَا مَتَاعٌ وَخَيْرُ مَتَاعِ الدُّنْيَا الْمَرْأَةُ الصَّالِحَةُ}$$

"The world is provision and the best worldly provision is a righteous woman." (Muslim)

This signifies that we should be favouring an individual who is upon the Dīn (religion). This will entail the marriage to be full of happiness, blessings and true love.

Trust Assigned to Humans

$$\text{إِنَّا عَرَضْنَا الْأَمَانَةَ عَلَى السَّمٰوٰتِ وَالْأَرْضِ وَالْجِبَالِ فَأَبَيْنَ أَنْ يَحْمِلْنَهَا وَأَشْفَقْنَ مِنْهَا وَحَمَلَهَا الْإِنْسَانُ إِنَّهُ كَانَ ظَلُومًا جَهُولًا}$$

"Indeed, We offered the trust to the heavens and the earth and the mountains, but they declined to bear its burden and were afraid of it and man picked it up. Indeed he is unjust (to himself), ignorant (of the end)." (33:72)

The scholars of Tafsīr have commented that the meaning of the verse is,

$$\text{لَا إِيْمَانَ لِمَنْ لَا أَمَانَةَ لَهُ}$$

"He who does not keep his trusts has no faith." (Baihaqi)

The scholars of Tafsīr also comment that this Amānah (trust) could possibly refer to two things:
1. The Holy Qur'ān
2. The Dīn (religion)

However, the actual 'trust' is the one which Allāh ﷻ mentioned in Ālam Arwāh,

$$\text{اَلَسْتُ بِرَبِّكُمْ قَالُوْا بَلٰی}$$

"Am I not Your Lord? They replied, Indeed You are." (7:172)

Only mankind has been entrusted with the responsibility of upholding Imān (faith) because they have been granted free will - this means humans are responsible regarding all their actions and will have to give an account on the Day of Judgement regarding all their deeds.

When this trust was put forth to the heavens, earth and the mountains, they immediately declined to bear this burden due to lacking the characteristics of intellect. Allāh ﷻ hence gave mankind this trust to fulfil as He has provided them with the characteristics e.g. intellect to differentiate between right and wrong. The lamentable situation is that despite possessing intellect we are still heedless and neglectful of this trust.

An objection could be raised as to why the Jinns were not mentioned alongside mankind. The answer is that the Jinns have been referred to as a substitute. The main creation who are responsible are the humans, followed by the Jinns.

ظَلُومًا and جَهُولًا are both hyperbolic participles. The word ظَلُومًا is used for that person who oppresses yet has the ability to command with justice. The word جَهُولًا is used for a person who is ignorant yet has the capability to acquire knowledge.

Lesson: We should always be grateful to Allāh ﷻ that He has gifted and blessed us with Imān (faith). We should constantly remember the accountability in front of Allāh ﷻ and also keep in mind the trust of Allāh ﷻ so that we become successful in the Hereafter.

Other titles from JKN Publications

Your Questions Answered
An outstanding book written by Shaykh Mufti Saiful Islām. A very comprehensive yet simple Fatāwa book and a source of guidance that reaches out to a wider audience i.e. the English speaking Muslims. The reader will benefit from the various answers to questions based on the Laws of Islām relating to the beliefs of Islām, knowledge, Sunnah, pillars of Islām, marriage, divorce and contemporary issues.

UK RRP: £7.50

Hadeeth for Beginners
A concise Hadeeth book with various Ahādeeth that relate to basic Ibādāh and moral etiquettes in Islām accessible to a wider readership. Each Hadeeth has been presented with the Arabic text, its translation and commentary to enlighten the reader, its meaning and application in day-to-day life.

UK RRP: £3.00

Du'ā for Beginners
This book contains basic Du'ās which every Muslim should recite on a daily basis. Highly recommended to young children and adults studying at Islamic schools and Madrasahs so that one may cherish the beautiful treasure of supplications of our beloved Prophet ﷺ in one's daily life, which will ultimately bring peace and happiness in both worlds, Inshā-Allāh.

UK RRP: £2.00

How well do you know Islām?
An exciting educational book which contains 300 multiple questions and answers to help you increase your knowledge on Islām! Ideal for the whole family, especially children and adult students to learn new knowledge in an enjoyable way and cherish the treasures of knowledge that you will acquire from this book. A very beneficial tool for educational syllabus.

UK RRP: £3.00

Treasures of the Holy Qur'ān
This book entitled "Treasures of the Holy Qur'ān" has been compiled to create a stronger bond between the Holy Qur'ān and the readers. It mentions the different virtues of Sūrahs and verses from the Holy Qur'ān with the hope that the readers will increase their zeal and enthusiasm to recite and inculcate the teachings of the Holy Qur'ān into their daily lives.

UK RRP: £3.00

Marriage - A Complete Solution
Islām regards marriage as a great act of worship. This book has been designed to provide the fundamental teachings and guidelines of all what relates to the marital life in a simplified English language. It encapsulates in a nutshell all the marriage laws mentioned in many of the main reference books in order to facilitate their understanding and implementation.

UK RRP: £5.00

Pearls of Luqmān
This book is a comprehensive commentary of Sūrah Luqmān, written beautifully by Shaykh Mufti Saiful Islām. It offers the reader with an enquiring mind, abundance of advice, guidance, counselling and wisdom.

The reader will be enlightened by many wonderful topics and anecdotes mentioned in this book, which will create a greater understanding of the Holy Qur'ān and its wisdom. The book highlights some of the wise sayings and words of advice Luqmān ※ gave to his son.

UK RRP: £3.00

Arabic Grammar for Beginners
This book is a study of Arabic Grammar based on the subject of Nahw (Syntax) in a simplified English format. If a student studies this book thoroughly, he/she will develop a very good foundation in this field, Inshā-Allāh. Many books have been written on this subject in various languages such as Arabic, Persian and Urdu. However, in this day and age there is a growing demand for this subject to be available in English .

UK RRP: £3.00

A Gift to My Youngsters
This treasure filled book, is a collection of Islamic stories, morals and anecdotes from the life of our beloved Prophet ﷺ, his Companions ※ and the pious predecessors. The stories and anecdotes are based on moral and ethical values, which the reader will enjoy sharing with their peers, friends, families and loved ones.

"A Gift to My Youngsters" – is a wonderful gift presented to the readers personally, by the author himself, especially with the youngsters in mind. He has carefully selected stories and anecdotes containing beautiful morals, lessons and valuable knowledge and wisdom.

UK RRP: £5.00

Travel Companion

The beauty of this book is that it enables a person on any journey, small or distant or simply at home, to utilise their spare time to read and benefit from an exciting and vast collection of important and interesting Islamic topics and lessons. Written in simple and easy to read text, this book will immensely benefit both the newly interested person in Islām and the inquiring mind of a student expanding upon their existing knowledge. Inspiring reminders from the Holy Qur'ān and the blessed words of our beloved Prophet ﷺ beautifies each topic and will illuminate the heart of the reader. **UK RRP: £5.00**

Pearls of Wisdom

Junaid Baghdādi ؓ once said, "Allāh ﷻ strengthens through these Islamic stories the hearts of His friends, as proven from the Qur'anic verse, **"And all that We narrate unto you of the stories of the Messengers, so as to strengthen through it your heart." (11:120)**
Mālik Ibn Dinār ؓ stated that such stories are gifts from Paradise. He also emphasised to narrate these stories as much as possible as they are gems and it is possible that an individual might find a truly rare and invaluable gem among them. **UK RRP: £6.00**

Inspirations

This book contains a compilation of selected speeches delivered by Shaykh Mufti Saiful Islām on a variety of topics such as the Holy Qur'ān, Nikāh and eating Halāl. Having previously been compiled in separate booklets, it was decided that the transcripts be gathered together in one book for the benefit of the reader. In addition to this, we have included in this book, further speeches which have not yet been printed.

UK RRP: £6.00

Gift to my Sisters

A thought provoking compilation of very interesting articles including real life stories of pious predecessors, imaginative illustrations and much more. All designed to influence and motivate mothers, sisters, wives and daughters towards an ideal Islamic lifestyle. A lifestyle referred to by our Creator, Allāh ﷻ in the Holy Qur'ān as the means to salvation and ultimate success.

UK RRP: £6.00

Gift to my Brothers

A thought provoking compilation of very interesting articles including real life stories of pious predecessors, imaginative illustrations, medical advices on intoxicants and rehabilitation and much more. All designed to influence and motivate fathers, brothers, husbands and sons towards an ideal Islamic lifestyle. A lifestyle referred to by our Creator, Allāh ﷻ in the Holy Qur'ān as the means to salvation and ultimate success.

UK RRP: £5.00

Heroes of Islām
"In the narratives there is certainly a lesson for people of intelligence (understanding)." (12:111)
A fine blend of Islamic personalities who have been recognised for leaving a lasting mark in the hearts and minds of people.
A distinguishing feature of this book is that the author has selected not only some of the most world and historically famous renowned scholars but also these lesser known and a few who have simply left behind a valuable piece of advice to their nearest and dearest.
UK RRP: £5.00

Ask a Mufti (3 volumes)
Muslims in every generation have confronted different kinds of challenges. In-spite of that, Islām produced such luminary Ulamā who confronted and responded to the challenges of their time to guide the Ummah to the straight path. "Ask A Mufti" is a comprehensive three volume fatwa book, based on the Hanafi School, covering a wide range of topics related to every aspect of human life such as belief, ritual worship, life after death and contemporary legal topics related to purity, commercial transaction, marriage, divorce, food, cosmetic, laws pertaining to women, Islamic medical ethics and much more.
UK RRP: £30.00

Should I Follow a Madhab?
Taqleed or following one of the four legal schools is not a new phenomenon. Historically, scholars of great calibre and luminaries, each one being a specialist in his own right, were known to have adhered to one of the four legal schools. It is only in the previous century that a minority group emerged advocating a severe ban on following one of the four major schools.
This book endeavours to address the topic of Taqleed and elucidates its importance and necessity in this day and age. It will also, by the Divine Will of Allāh ﷻ dispel some of the confusion surrounding this topic.
UK RRP: £5.00

Advice for the Students of Knowledge
Allāh ﷻ describes divine knowledge in the Holy Qur'ān as a 'Light'. Amongst the qualities of light are purity and guidance. The Holy Prophet ﷺ has clearly explained this concept in many blessed Ahādeeth and has also taught us many supplications in which we ask for beneficial knowledge.
This book is a golden tool for every sincere student of knowledge wishing to mould his/her character and engrain those correct qualities in order to be worthy of receiving the great gift of Ilm from Allāh ﷻ.
UK RRP: £3.00

Stories for Children
"Stories for Children" - is a wonderful gift presented to the readers personally by the author himself, especially with the young children in mind. The stories are based on moral and ethical values, which the reader will enjoy sharing with their peers, friends, families and loved ones. The aim is to present to the children stories and incidents which contain moral lessons, in order to reform and correct their lives, according to the Holy Qur'ān and Sunnah.
UK RRP: £5.00

Pearls from My Shaykh
This book contains a collection of pearls and inspirational accounts of the Holy Prophet ﷺ, his noble Companions, pious predecessors and some personal accounts and sayings of our well-known contemporary scholar and spiritual guide, Shaykh Mufti Saiful Islām Sāhib. Each anecdote and narrative of the pious predecessors have been written in the way that was narrated by Mufti Saiful Islām Sāhib in his discourses, drawing the specific lessons he intended from telling the story. The accounts from the life of the Shaykh has been compiled by a particular student based on their own experience and personal observation. **UK RRP: £5.00**

Paradise & Hell
This book is a collection of detailed explanation of Paradise and Hell including the state and conditions of its inhabitants. All the details have been taken from various reliable sources. The purpose of its compilation is for the reader to contemplate and appreciate the innumerable favours, rewards, comfort and unlimited luxuries of Paradise and at the same time take heed from the punishment of Hell. Shaykh Mufti Saiful Islām Sāhib has presented this book in a unique format by including the Tafseer and virtues of Sūrah Ar-Rahmān. **UK RRP: £5.00**

Prayers for Forgiveness
Prayers for Forgiveness' is a short compilation of Du'ās in Arabic with English translation and transliteration. This book can be studied after 'Du'ā for Beginners' or as a separate book. It includes twenty more Du'ās which have not been mentioned in the previous Du'ā book. It also includes a section of Du'ās from the Holy Qur'ān and a section from the Ahādeeth. The book concludes with a section mentioning the Ninety-Nine Names of Allāh ﷻ with its translation and transliteration. **UK RRP: £3.00**

Scattered Pearls
This book is a collection of scattered pearls taken from books, magazines, emails and WhatsApp messages. These pearls will hopefully increase our knowledge, wisdom and make us realise the purpose of life. In this book, Mufti Sāhib has included messages sent to him from scholars, friends and colleagues which will be beneficial and interesting for our readers Inshā-Allāh. **UK RRP: £4.00**

Poems of Wisdom
This book is a collection of poems from those who contributed to the Al-Mumin Magazine in the poems section. The Hadeeth mentions "Indeed some form of poems are full of wisdom." The themes of each poem vary between wittiness, thought provocation, moral lessons, emotional to name but a few. The readers will benefit from this immensely and make them ponder over the outlook of life in general.

UK RRP: £4.00

Horrors of Judgement Day
This book is a detailed and informative commentary of the first three Sūrahs of the last Juz namely; Sūrah Naba, Sūrah Nāzi'āt and Sūrah Abasa. These Sūrahs vividly depict the horrific events and scenes of the Great Day in order to warn mankind the end of this world. These Sūrahs are an essential reminder for us all to instil the fear and concern of the Day of Judgement and to detach ourselves from the worldly pleasures. Reading this book allows us to attain the true realization of this world and provides essential advices of how to gain eternal salvation in the Hereafter.
RRP: £5:00

Spiritual Heart
It is necessary that Muslims always strive to better themselves at all times and to free themselves from the destructive maladies. This book focusses on three main spiritual maladies; pride, anger and evil gazes. It explains its root causes and offers some spiritual cures. Many examples from the lives of the pious predecessors are used for inspiration and encouragement for controlling the above three maladies. It is hoped that the purification process of the heart becomes easy once the underlying roots of the above maladies are clearly understood. **UK RRP: £5:00**

Hajj & Umrah for Beginners
This book is a step by step guide on Hajj and Umrah for absolute beginners. Many other additional important rulings (Masāil) have been included that will Insha-Allāh prove very useful for our readers. The book also includes some etiquettes of visiting (Ziyārat) of the Holy Prophet's ﷺ blessed Masjid and his Holy Grave.
UK RRP £3:00

Advice for the Spiritual Travellers
This book contains essential guidelines for a spiritual Murīd to gain some familiarity of the science of Tasawwuf. It explains the meaning and aims of Tasawwuf, some understanding around the concept of the soul, and general guidelines for a spiritual Murīd. This is highly recommended book and it is hoped that it gains wider readership among those Murīds who are basically new to the science of Tasawwuf.
UK RRP £3:00

Don't Worry Be Happy
This book is a compilation of sayings and earnest pieces of advice that have been gathered directly from my respected teacher Shaykh Mufti Saiful Islām Sāhib. The book consists of many valuable enlightenments including how to deal with challenges of life, promoting unity, practicing good manners, being optimistic and many other valuable advices. Our respected Shaykh has gathered this Naseehah from meditating, contemplating, analysing and searching for the gems within Qur'anic verses, Ahādeeth and teachings of our Pious Predecessors. **UK RRP £1:00**

Kanzul Bāri
Kanzul Bāri provides a detailed commentary of the Ahādeeth contained in Saheeh al-Bukhāri. The commentary includes Imām Bukhāri's ﷺ biography, the status of his book, spiritual advice, inspirational accounts along with academic discussions related to Fiqh, its application and differences of opinion. Moreover, it answers objections arising in one's mind about certain Ahādeeth. Inquisitive students of Hadeeth will find this commentary a very useful reference book in the final year of their Ālim course for gaining a deeper understanding of the science of Hadeeth. **UK RRP: £15.00**

How to Become a Friend of Allāh ﷻ
The friends of Allāh ﷻ have been described in detail in the Holy Qur'ān and Āhadeeth. This book endeavours its readers to help create a bond with Allāh ﷻ in attaining His friendship as He is the sole Creator of all material and immaterial things. It is only through Allāh's ﷻ friendship, an individual will achieve happiness in this life and the Hereafter, hence eliminate worries, sadness, depression, anxiety and misery of this world. **UK RRP:**

Gems & Jewels
This book contains a selection of articles which have been gathered for the benefit of the readers covering a variety of topics on various aspects of daily life. It offers precious advice and anecdotes that contain moral lessons. The advice captivates its readers and will extend the narrowness of their thoughts to deep reflection, wisdom and appreciation of the purpose of our existence. **UK RRP: £4.00**

End of Time
This book is a comprehensive explanation of the three Sūrahs of Juzz Amma; Sūrah Takweer, Sūrah Infitār and Sūrah Mutaffifeen. This book is a continuation from the previous book of the same author, 'Horrors of Judgement Day'. The three Sūrahs vividly sketch out the scene of the Day of Judgement and describe the state of both the inmates of Jannah and Jahannam. Mufti Saiful Islām Sāhib provides an easy but comprehensive commentary of the three Sūrahs facilitating its understanding for the readers whilst capturing the horrific scene of the ending of the world and the conditions of mankind on that horrific Day. **UK RRP: £5.00**

Andalus (modern day Spain), the long lost history, was once a country that produced many great calibre of Muslim scholars comprising of Mufassirūn, Muhaddithūn, Fuqahā, judges, scientists, philosophers, surgeons, to name but a few. The Muslims conquered Andalus in 711 AD and ruled over it for eight-hundred years. This was known as the era of Muslim glory. Many non-Muslim Europeans during that time travelled to Spain to study under Muslim scholars. The remanences of the Muslim rule in Spain are manifested through their universities, magnificent palaces and Masājid carved with Arabic writings, standing even until today. In this book, Shaykh Mufti Saiful Islām shares some of his valuable experiences he witnessed during his journey to Spain. **UK RRP: £3.00**

Ideal Youth
This book contains articles gathered from various social media avenues; magazines, emails, WhatsApp and telegram messages that provide useful tips of advice for those who have the zeal to learn and consider changing their negative habits and behavior and become better Muslims to set a positive trend for the next generation. **UK RRP:£4:00**

Ideal Teacher
This book contains abundance of precious advices for the Ulamā who are in the teaching profession. It serves to present Islamic ethical principles of teaching and to remind every teacher of their moral duties towards their students. This book will Inshā-Allāh prove to be beneficial for newly graduates and scholars wanting to utilize their knowledge through teaching. **UK RRP:£4:00**

Ideal Student
This book is a guide for all students of knowledge in achieving the excellent qualities of becoming an ideal student. It contains precious advices, anecdotes of our pious predecessors and tips in developing good morals as a student. Good morals is vital for seeking knowledge. A must for all students if they want to develop their Islamic Knowledge. **UK RRP:£4:00**

Ideal Parents
This book contains a wealth of knowledge in achieving the qualities of becoming ideal parents. It contains precious advices, anecdotes of our pious predecessors and tips in developing good parenthood skills. Good morals is vital for seeking knowledge. A must for all parents. **UK RRP:£4:00**

Ideal Couple
This book is a compilation of inspiring stories and articles containing useful tips and life skills for every couple. Marriage life is a big responsibility and success in marriage is only possible if the couple know what it means to be an ideal couple. **UK RRP:£4:00**

Ideal Role Model
This book is a compilation of sayings and accounts of our pious predecessors. The purpose of this book is so we can learn from our pious predecessors the purpose of this life and how to attain closer to the Creator. Those people who inspires us attaining closeness to our Creator are our true role models. A must everyone to read. **UK RRP:£4:00**

Ideal Role Model
This book is a compilation of sayings and accounts of our pious predecessors. The purpose of this book is so we can learn from our pious predecessors the purpose of this life and how to attain closer to the Creator. Those people who inspires us attaining closeness to our Creator are our true role models. A must everyone to read. **UK RRP:£4:00**

Bangladesh- A Land of Natural Beauty
This book is a compilation of our respected Shaykh's journeys to Bangladesh including visits to famous Madāris and Masājid around the country. The Shaykh shares some of his thought provoking experiences and his personal visits with great scholars in Bangladesh.
UK RRP: £4.00

Pearls from the Qur'an
This series begins with the small Sūrahs from 30th Juzz initially, unravelling its heavenly gems, precious advices and anecdotes worthy of personal reflection. It will most definitely benefit both those new to as well as advanced students of the science of Tafsīr. The purpose is to make it easily accessible for the general public in understanding the meaning of the Holy Qur'ān. **UK RRP: £10.00**

When the Heavens Split
This book contains the commentary of four Sūrahs from Juzz Amma namely; Sūrah Inshiqāq, Sūrah Burūj, Sūrah Tāriq and Sūrah A'lā. The first two Sūrahs contain a common theme of capturing the scenes and events of the Last Day and how this world will come to an end. However, all four Sūrahs mentioned, have a connection of the journey of humanity, reflection on nature, how nature changes and most importantly, giving severe warnings to mankind about the punishments and exhorting them to prepare for the Hereafter through good deeds and refraining from sins.
UK RRP: £4.00

The Lady who Spoke the Qur'ān
The Holy Prophet ﷺ was sent as a role model who was the physical form of the Holy Qur'ān. Following the ways of the Holy Prophet ﷺ in every second of our lives is pivotal for success. This booklet tells us the way to gain this success. It also includes an inspirational incident of an amazing lady who only spoke from the Holy Qur'an throughout her life. We will leave it to our readers to marvel at her intelligence, knowledge and piety expressed in this breath-taking episode.
UK RRP:£3:00

Dearest Act to Allāh
Today our Masājid have lofty structures, engraved brickworks, exquisite chandeliers and laid rugs, but they are spiritually deprived due to the reason that the Masājid are used for social purposes including backbiting and futile talk rather than the performance of Salāh, Qur'ān recitation and the spreading of true authentic Islamic knowledge. This book elaborates on the etiquettes of the Masjid and the importance of Salāh with Quranic and prophetic proofs along with some useful anecdotes to emphasize their importance. **UK RRP:£3:00**

Don't Delay Your Nikāh
Marriage plays an important role in our lives. It is a commemoration of the union of two strangers who will spend the rest of their remaining lives with one another. Marriage ought to transpire comfort and tranquillity whereby the couple share one another's sorrow and happiness. It is strongly recommended that our brothers and sisters read and benefit from this book and try to implement it into our daily lives in order to once more revive the Sunnah of the Holy Prophet ﷺ on such occasions and repel the prevalent sins and baseless customs.

UK RRP:£3:00

Miracle of the Holy Qur'ān
The scholars of Islām are trying to wake us all up, however, we are busy dreaming of the present world and have forgotten our real destination. Shaykh Mufti Saiful Islām Sāhib has been conducted Tafsīr of the Holy Qur'ān every week for almost two decades with the purpose of reviving its teachings and importance. This book is a transcription of two titles; Miracle of the Holy Qur'ān and The Revelation of the Holy Qur'ān, both delivered during the weekly Tafsīr sessions.
UK RRP:£3:00

You are what you Eat
Eating Halāl and earning a lawful income plays a vital role in the acceptance of all our Ibādāt (worship) and good deeds. Mufti Saiful Islām Sāhib has presented a discourse on this matter in one of his talks. I found the discourse to be very beneficial, informative and enlightening on the subject of Halāl and Harām that clarifies its importance and status in Islām. I strongly recommend my Muslim brothers and sisters to read this treatise and to study it thoroughly.

UK RRP:£3:00

Sleepers of the Cave
The Tafsīr of Sūrah Kahf is of crucial importance in this unique and challenging time we are currently living in. This book is evidently beneficial for all Muslims, more crucial for the general public. This is because Mufti Sāhib gives us extensive advice on how to act accordingly when treading the path of seeking knowledge. Readers will find amazing pieces of advice in terms of etiquettes regarding seeking knowledge and motivation, Inshā-Allāh. **UK RRP:£5:00**

Contentment of the Heart
The purification of the soul and its rectification are matters of vital importance which were brought by our Holy Prophet e to this Ummah. The literal meaning of Tazkiyah is 'to cleanse'. The genuine Sūfis assert that the foundation and core of all virtuous character is sincerity and the basis for all evil characteristics and traits is love for this world. This book endeavors to address certain spiritual maladies and how to overcome them using Islamic principles. **UK RRP:£5:00**

Contemporary Fiqh
This book is a selection of detailed *Fiqhi* (juridical) articles on contemporary legal issues. These detailed articles provide an in depth and elaborative response to some of the queries posted to us in our Fatawa department over the last decade. The topics discussed range between purity, domestic issues, Halāl and Harām, Islamic medical ethics, marital issues, rituals and so forth. Many of the juristic cases are unprecedented as a result of the ongoing societal changes and newly arising issues. **UK RRP:£6:00**

Ideal Society
In this book, 'Ideal Society' which is a commentary of Sūrah Hujurāt, Shaykh Mufti Saiful Islām Sāhib explains the lofty status of our beloved Prophet ﷺ, the duties of the believers and general mankind and how to live a harmonious social life, which is free from evil, jealousy and vices. Inshā-Allāh, this book will enable and encourage the readers to adopt a social life which will ultimately bring happiness and joy to each and every individual.

UK RRP:£5:00